Happy Birthday
to my own needlepoint
teacher — Sylvia —
you really started
something.

LOVE

Diana

# NEEDLEPOINT RUGS

BOOKS BY HOPE HANLEY

*NEEDLEPOINT*

*NEW METHODS IN NEEDLEPOINT*

*NEEDLEPOINT IN AMERICA*

*NEEDLEPOINT RUGS*

# Needlepoint Rugs

by HOPE HANLEY

CHARLES SCRIBNER'S SONS • *New York*

PRINTED IN THE UNITED STATES OF AMERICA
Library of Congress Catalog Card Number 77-162728

SBN 684-12484-X

FRONTIS. A tiny warp cloth rug worked in bargello patterns in three shades of turquoise. The light background is the plain weave of the warp cloth. The inspiration for the design comes from the Turkoman rug illustration on page 105.

*Dedicated to*
*DORIS W. THOMPSON,*
*who was an expert on*
*needlepoint and courage.*

# PREFACE

In today's mass-produced world of sterile design, more people are turning to handwork, not only to create an original and personal design, but also for the pride of achievement. The increased interest in needlepoint rugs probably stems from this creative need. Needlepoint has an extra quality, a therapeutic one. The process of working stitch after stitch has a soothing effect on jangled nerves. It is my hope that this book will increase your enjoyment of the craft as well as gently guide you around some of its pitfalls.

The outline of the book progresses along the same line of thinking that you will follow in planning and making your rug. It starts with design ideas and then attention is focused on the kinds of wools and canvas that are available. Various stitches suitable for rugs come next. The different methods and mediums for applying the design to the canvas follow. After that come chapters on joining the pieces of the rug, blocking it and the finishing touches.

# CONTENTS

# ACKNOWLEDGMENTS

There is no way to thank adequately all the wonderful people who helped me gather information and illustrations for this book. All I can do is to state that it is their contributions, which put together, make the book. Without such grand people my job would be very, very hard. Again I am deeply in debt to Miss Doris Bowman of the Smithsonian Institution, to Mr. James M. O'Neill of the District of Columbia Public Library, and to Mrs. Thomas P. Dillon, of Washington, D. C.

Three Washington area shops were most helpful in contributing information on materials, both domestic and imported. My thanks go to Mrs. Walter Surrey of The Elegant Needle, to Mrs. G. Howland Chase of the American Needlework Center as well as Mrs. Joanna Huntington Noel, and to Mrs. Inez Fowler of the Hook, Braid N" Needle Crafts Center. There were three people on whom I called whenever I needed advice, and they are Rosetta Larsen of New York, Mrs. Dorothy Burchette of Rockville, Maryland, and Mr. Louis J. Gartner of Palm Beach, Florida. Mrs. J. Alton Boyer made a rug for her sister so that we could "learn by doing." Mrs. Richard E. Riegel, Jr. arranged a whirlwind tour of Wilmington, Delaware, to find rugs to photograph. Mr. Anthony Landreau of The Textile Museum of Washington, D. C. was very helpful in a related field, flat-woven rugs. But the people on whom I leaned the very hardest are my sweet daughter, Lee, and my favorite editor, Elinor Parker.

# NEEDLEPOINT RUGS

# 1. Design Ideas and Considerations

THE FACTORS that affect the designing of a needlepoint rug are the same ones that affect your choice when buying a rug. In what room do you want to use the rug, what style do you want it to be, how much space must it cover? What colors will be suitable in this particular area? The need for durability or the lack will influence the choice of canvas and wool and to some extent, color. A "special effect"

OPPOSITE. An oriental-style prayer rug worked on rug canvas by Doctor Earle Silber. It is used as a wall hanging.

rug might be worked in rug wool because it stitches up faster. For heirloom quality you might be willing to invest more time and so would choose finer wool and canvas. Do you want to "pick up" a floor area? If so, then a lighter colored rug is in order, darker colors will hold the area down.

Another consideration is just how portable you want the making of the rug to be. If most of your stitching will be done on the run, small pieces would be best; you could work a large piece in a floor frame if you expect to stitch at home.

A visit to the library will provide you with many design ideas. Draw out books on oriental rugs, interior decorating picture books, and historic houses books. From the oriental rug books you will see that abstract designs, seemingly clashing colors and busy busy patterns look fine even together. The interior decorating books will show you what colors seem to stay on the floor best and that simplicity might be the wisest course. The historic houses books will show you what fits in best with your style of decor.

Your interests, likes and hobbies are a great source of ideas. If you like wild flowers, postage stamps, ferns or fish, by all means, draw on that idea. Two books which may inspire you are *Handbook of Decorative Design and Ornament* by Mary Jean Alexander, and *Handbook of Designs and Motifs* by P. J. Tomajan, both published by Tudor Publishing Company, New York. From such a book one could choose one small motif and repeat it in an even pattern, but varying the colors, which in turn creates a larger pattern. Or one could take one large geometric design and put different color stripes behind it. When using small motifs, make sure the design is big enough to be seen. Think of a calico quilt laid on the floor as an example of too small a pattern.

Books on stained glass offer a variety of motifs, particularly the windows of the twelfth to the fourteenth century. Details taken from the window borders translate into needlepoint quite well. The "leads" would not necessarily have to be black, they could be the background color of the rug. Architectural details, such as arches and columns, are good subject matter for rugs. Woven coverlet patterns are already blocked out, ready to be used. For those people who think that they can't draw or have no sense of design a map done in outline would be easy. Simple landmarks could be shown which mean something to the individual.

Persian and Indian art provide endless striking flower and tree designs. The Victoria and Albert Museum in England has a 17th century Indian rug that has a design of wild flowers each placed in a separate space in a chicken-wire-like framework, and all of it set in a plain border.

Bargello patterns could be used for rugs by simply doing half-cross stitches in rows or brick stitches instead of four mesh long

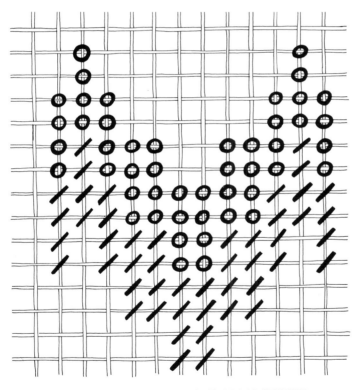

BARGELLO-TYPE IN HALF CROSS STITCH

stitches. At the Dwight-Barnard House in Deerfield, Massachusetts, there is a lovely flame stitch rug with a simple striped border. A darker color than the main background color of the rug seems to give the most finished look to rug borders. Some oriental rug designs splash over into the border, thus making it look less confining.

As a general rule, figurative rugs seem to belong in children's rooms, or the den or library. Adapting curtain material or upholstery material to rug design is a risky business. The making of a rug is apt

The placement of the fish on the rug facing page 8 was decided by the use of these paper cut-outs. The tiny fish were moved about until the design was pleasing and then glued in place.

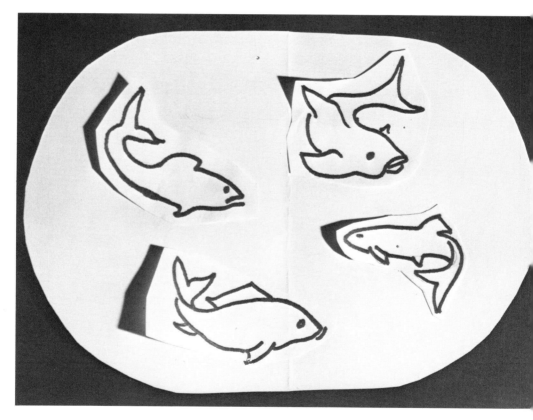

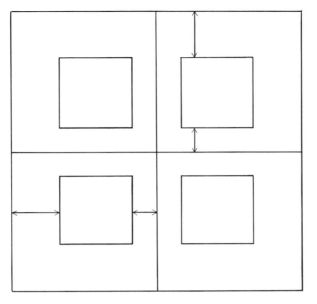

The inside borders must be half the measurement of the outside border.

to be a lengthy process and the material may be worn out by the time you finish it, or you may be tired of the material and want to make a change.

Some people have great designing talent and can just dash off a perfect design the first try, while the rest of us need little helps and crutches. Here are a few. Having decided on the general size and shape of your rug, make a few preliminary sketches of the design you have in mind. If you are having trouble with the arrangement of the motifs or figures, trace off a few of each motif and cut them out. Then simply move them about until you find the most pleasing design. Glue will hold them in place while you lay a piece of tracing paper over the design to record it.

If you are designing a geometric rug it helps if you work from the center of the pattern out to the edges. If you are making a pieced rug and plan a border on each piece, the outside edges of the rug should have a border twice the width of the inside borders. Thus, if your inside borders are to be an inch wide, when they are joined they will make a two inch wide border. Therefore your outside edge borders should be two inches to match them. Sketching this kind of rug out on graph paper, letting one square equal an inch or whatever you decide will help figuring out this border business.

Having decided on the layout of your design some consideration must be given to the details of color and shading. Do you plan to outline each figure coloring-book-style or are you going to use color hard edge against hard edge? How much shading do you plan to use, if any? One way to beg the question of shading and outlining is to outline each color in a lighter or darker shade of the same color. Thus a petal will have two shades of pink on it, a leaf two shades of green. This gives a slightly shaded effect and takes away a little of the coloring-book look. If you plan a lot of shading it can be painted in when you come to painting the canvas. Shading is easier to do on a finer mesh canvas because there are more mesh to cover. Flat coloring or very simple shading is more appropriate for large mesh canvas. Your design more or less dictates what size canvas to use, or if you choose your canvas first, the canvas decides how elaborate a design to use.

OPPOSITE, TOP. These charming animals were adapted from greeting card designs. The rug was made on ten mesh mono-canvas in separate squares, the border is cross stitched. OWNED BY MR. AND MRS. ARMANDO RODRIGUEZ OF WASHINGTON, D. C.

OPPOSITE, BOTTOM. A small rug made on ten mesh canvas with Persian yarn. The fish are done each in a different stitch, the knit stitch, the brick stitch, the mosaic and the mosaic stitch done diagonally were those used. The fish were traced from wildlife and children's books and then the tracings were simplified. See page 6.

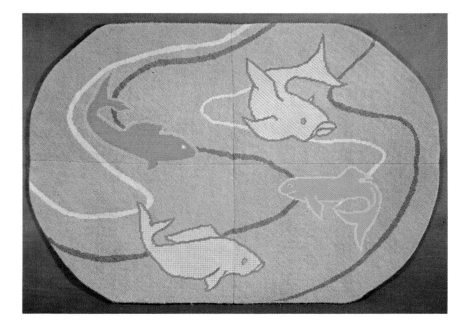

# 2. Rug Materials

## CANVAS

Most people want durability when choosing a rug canvas. A light cross stitch-type canvas will just not stand up to much wear; if you can rip the canvas bare-handed, it is too fragile to use. Rugs are usually worked on large meshed canvases, ranging from ten mesh to the inch canvas down to three and a half mesh per inch, with the corresponding wools. Any canvas will do if it is sturdy enough. Pictured below are some of the usual canvases used for rugs.

Mono-canvas is a hard twisted cotton thread canvas which is available in fourteen, twelve, ten and seven mesh to the inch. Ten mesh is the most suitable for rugs. It is white or ecru in color, and comes in rolls about forty inches wide. Occasionally it can be found fifty-four inches wide; this is a difficult length to store which might explain why it is not always available. Once people have tried mono-canvas it is preferred over two-thread because it is easier on the eyes. Shops prefer it because it is easier to paint on. There is one drawback to using mono-canvas for rugs, it is harder to join than the two-thread canvases. The single thread of mono-canvas is considerable thicker than the two-thread and does not handle as well in four-piece joins. This is not to say it cannot be done well, it just takes a little more patience and practice. One strand of tapestry yarn works well on ten mesh mono-canvas and one strand of the three thread Persian or Colbert Six fits this canvas too.

Penelope canvas is a two thread canvas with its warp threads set in close pairs and its weft threads in pairs slightly wider apart.

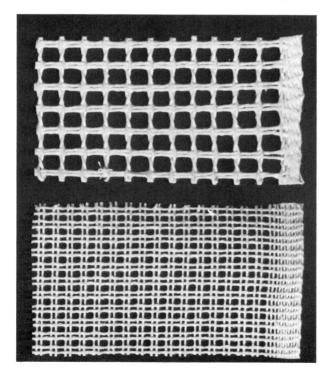

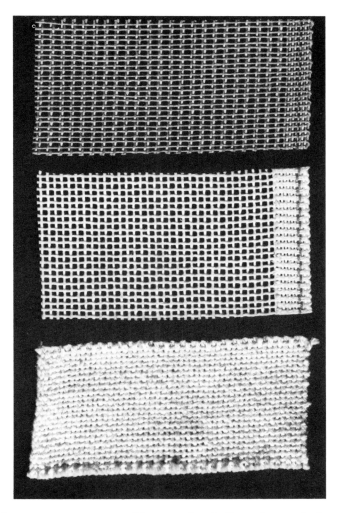

Canvases suitable for rug use. OPPOSITE. Three and a half mesh per inch, five mesh rug canvas. ABOVE, TOP TO BOTTOM. Seven mesh penelope, ten mesh mono-canvas, and last, fourteen threads to the inch warp cloth.

It is usually ecru in color and comes in seven and ten mesh to the inch. The paired threads can be separated, resulting in a fine mono-canvas, thus a seven mesh penelope canvas could have its details worked in fourteen mesh mono-canvas. The seven mesh is extremely satisfactory for rugs; two strands of tapestry, or two strands of the three thread wools or one strand of Shag-Rug cover it very well in half cross stitch.

Rug canvas or two thread canvas comes in five, four and three and a half mesh per inch. The larger mesh canvases are more heavily sized and so are rougher on the hands; however, the work goes much faster because there are relatively fewer mesh to fill. Two thread canvas is usually available in forty inch width though some shops carry a five mesh canvas that is seventy-two inches wide. The five mesh and the four and a half mesh are made in yellow or white, the white is to be preferred. The yellow color, riding the sizing, sometimes runs when the canvas is wet. Before working any of the rug canvases it is a very good practice to thoroughly wet a small swatch of it to see if the color runs and to see how much of the sizing comes out. You want a canvas that retains most of its sizing so that it will not become limp after blocking. The three and a half mesh canvas is white and the most highly sized of them all. It is a leno weave, which means that two warp threads cross each other before they accept a new weft thread. To a needlepointer, this means that the canvas cannot be split down to be used as a smaller meshed mono-canvas, the leno twist prevents it.

Warp cloth is not truly a canvas but it can be used for rugs. It is an even weave material with a soft string-like thread of four ply firmly twisted together. Because it has no sizing it crushes down, making it easy to work on. It must be firmly lined and is more suitable for small scatter rugs than a major project. The half cross stitch does not fit well on warp cloth because of its thick threads and small holes, but it works very well for bargello and other large stitches. Warp cloth comes in a heavy seven mesh weight in rolls of forty inches wide and seventy-two inches wide; the lighter approximately fourteen mesh per inch weight comes only in the seventy-two inch width. Make sure that the warp cloth that you buy has a firmly twisted thread. Some of them do not and your needle will pick up threads from other mesh. The Heirloom Needlework Guild product is quite

A one-piece rug worked by Mrs. G. Howland Chase of Washington, D. C. on five mesh rug canvas. The gull's eye was worked over ten mesh by separating the double thread canvas into mono-canvas.

good. A strand of Shag-Rug will work on the seven mesh cloth and two threads or a full strand of Persian or Colbert Six, depending on the stitch, will fit the fourteen mesh.

## WOOL

Paternayan Persian wool is probably the finest weight wool one would use on rugs. It has a long fiber which is what one wants in a rug yarn. It is a three thread two-ply strand that can be used whole or can be split down to use in other number combinations. It is available in four hundred colors.

A new wool similar in strand and weight to the Persian yarn is Colbert Six. It is Australian wool, spun and dyed in France by the Bon Pasteur Company of St. Epin. They have so far one hundred and fifty colors on their chart. This firm makes other kinds of needlework yarn including a rug yarn called Smyrna in seventy colors. At present it is available only on special order.

Tapestry wool is slightly heavier than the three thread yarn and is a four ply-twist. It is made by several companies in this country but it is hard to find a shop with more than just background-type colors. Needlecraft House of West Townsend, Massachusetts, has a fine tapestry yarn in a nice range of colors. Appleton of England has a selection of three hundred and fifty rather classic tapestry colors. A few shops carry it in this country or will order it for you. A Danish firm, O. Oehlenschlager, also known as OOE, makes a vividly colored line of tapestry yarns, a few shops stock it.

Paternayan rug wool is a fat three-ply yarn which fits the five mesh, four mesh and three and a half mesh rug canvas. The one hundred and eighty colors correspond to the Persian yarn colors. Paternayan has another rug yarn, coarser in texture than the "Pat-Rug" but of almost tapestry size. It is made for the rya-type rugs but can be used for needlepoint. It uses the same color card as the "Pat-Rug," and is called "Shag-Rug."

Spinnerin Yarn Company of New York for years has made a yarn used for rug hooking. It is slightly heavier in weight than tapestry yarn. Previously it was cut and packaged just for hooking. It is now packaged uncut in fifteen bright colors for needle-made rugs.

Berga of Sweden manufactures a very evenly spun and durable rya yarn. (Some rya yarns are unevenly spun and full of slubs.) Their color card has over 140 colors on it. This type of wool would be useful for the less formal type of rug.

OOE's rug yarn is called Sudan Garn and is more loosely spun than American rug yarns. It seems to fit a seven mesh canvas better than the five mesh. It comes in eighty-five earthy colors. Needlecraft House imports a good quality New Zealand wool which is spun and

Samples of wool suitable for rug making. The three stranded piece is Persian wool, the next is tapestry, then Shag-Rug, and the last is rug wool. Numbers 18 and 14 needles may be used with the finer wools, a small rug needle may be used with the rug wool. The large two and three-quarters inch rug needles are too unwieldly to use except on the three and a half mesh canvas.

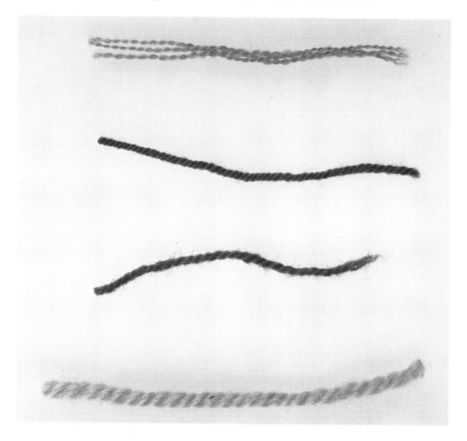

dyed in New England in twenty-one bright colors. It covers five mesh canvas nicely.

The Nantucket Needleworks in Nantucket, Massachusetts, imports and then dyes a cabled rug yarn. It feels quite hard but is easy to work with. It now comes in over fifty colors. Bernat's of Boston has a new acrylic washable rug yarn which they hope eventually to produce in over fifty colors. It is quite inexpensive. It has not been on the market long enough to measure its durability.

Rather than try to remember what number needle goes with which canvas, just remember that if the needle and wool slip through the canvas with ease, the needle fits. The needle and its load of wool should not spread the canvas threads as they pass through. Try a number 14 needle for rug wool, an 18 for tapestry wool and a 19 for Persian wool, full strand.

It is difficult to recommend the exact wool to use with each canvas because of the use of fancy stitches. One wool will cover a canvas very well in half cross stitch and not do at all well in another stitch. The only thing to do is to experiment and decide for yourself. Buy a quarter of a yard of the canvas you want to use for your rug, and four or five strands each of the colors of wool you want to use (if you can buy in small quantities). Make yourself some sample swatches not only of color combinations but stitch combinations. The quantity of wool and canvas needed for a rug is too great to run the risk of making an expensive mistake in purchasing. The sample swatches will help you figure wool quantities, give you a chance to practice joins if you are not making a strip rug, and help you decide if you can live with the colors you have selected. Just stitch around perhaps a three inch area at random, so that each color will touch all the others. No pattern is necessary. You'll be surprised how the

OPPOSITE. A small rug worked on seven mesh two-thread canvas with Berlin type wools in rusts, greens and roses. The rug was purchased in Frankfort in 1879 by Mrs. John Sevier. It was worked by Mrs. Sevier and Miss Louise A. Davidson of Bethesda, Maryland. Miss Davidson completed it in 1951.

A sampler showing the effect of various stitches; see key below.

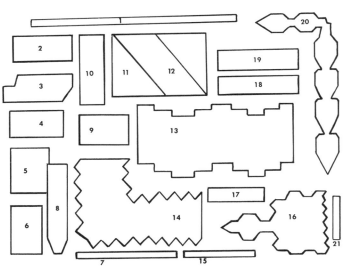

1. Soumak
2. Shell or sheath
3. Laced chain
4. Mosaic in 4's
5. Mosaic diagonal
6. Plain mosaic
7. Tramé Cross st.
8. Surrey and Turkey work
10. Herringbone in rows
11. Greek
12. Long armed cross diagonally
13. Bargello
14. Brick with a corner turn
15. Binding st. worked on the flat
16. Leaf in stripes
17. Knit
18. Herringbone
19. Herringbone reverse
20. Leaf and a corner turn
21. Two color Herringbone

colors react to each other, perhaps you will need some softer or brighter hues, or maybe less of a particularly loud one.

If the wool is too heavy for the canvas it will push the threads out of line. If it is too thin, it will not cover the canvas. Perhaps the stitch you have chosen will prove too tedious to work over a large area or twists the canvas too much. Even the best of wools occasionally run. Cut an inch or less of all the colors you want to use and lay them out on a paper towel. Drop a few drops of water on each sample and leave them for an hour. If any of them are going to run they will have left a stain on the paper towel. This is not an absolutely conclusive test, perhaps something else will make the color run, but at least you know the wool will not run during the blocking process.

You will find the preliminary testing on wool and canvas useful for another reason, that is, estimating how much wool you will need. Work a square inch on your chosen canvas of each stitch, having first measured the length of the strand you have in the needle. To figure the number of square inches your rug will be, multiply the length by the width in inches. Now multiply the inchage of the rug by the inchage of the wool you used. The resulting figure must be divided by thirty-six to get the yardage. You will have to "guesstimate" just how much each area will need of each color unless you wait until the canvas is painted and can measure exactly. It is better to have too much wool than too little because of dye lot difficulties. Most wools are pretty uniform from lot to lot and the variations are very slight, but they will show in large areas.

While you are contemplating canvases and wools some thought should be given to the kind of join you plan to use if you do not make a one-piece rug. For some joins one canvas is better than another. Chapter Four will show you the many different types of joins and the canvases for which they are best suited.

# 3. Stitches

CERTAIN qualities make some stitches more suitable for rug use than others. A good rug stitch does not distort the canvas. For instance, the continental stitch causes the canvas to lean to the right, the knotted stitch will make a canvas narrower, the encroaching Gobelin stitch will draw up the canvas and make it shorter. An embroidery frame will cure this problem nicely but if you don't want to use a frame, distorting stitches should be avoided. If you are in doubt about a stitch's wayward habits, a three- by three-inch sample should give you a clue.

A good rug stitch covers the canvas. Wear will thin your wool somewhat, so make sure the stitches you choose really cover. Very loose stitches, those that span many mesh at a stroke, have a tendency to show the canvas. They are also more apt to snag from nails in shoes, and buckles. If you have painted your canvas the fact that some shows is not so obvious. Keep a repair kit handy of the appropriate colors of wool when you finish the rug. You may have to replace some stitches some day.

One way to insure that the wool covers the canvas is to tramé the canvas first. Tramé is an under-stitching used to show the design to the needlepointer and to add richness and body to the design. On two thread canvas it is laid between the two threads, over a random number of mesh. (If it is laid in even rows it will form ridges which will show through the covering stitches.) Tramé can be used on mono-canvas only if you are going to work your stitches over two mesh.

A good rug stitch does not have more wool on the back of the

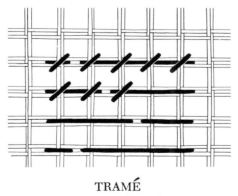

TRAMÉ
With half cross stitches indicated on the top rows

canvas than on the front. Even if you are using an inexpensive wool the sheer quantity needed to make a rug makes the cost somewhat high. Why waste the wool on the underside of the rug?

There is a lot of canvas to cover on a needlepoint rug and for this reason, many needlepointers turn to the fancier stitches. They are less monotonous to do than the half cross stitch, they work up faster and they add texture to your work. One can add too much texture so that the viewer is more conscious of the stitches than of the overall effect. Experience will show you that more than three or four fancy stitches per rug will give a very "artsy-craftsy" look to your work. Your subject matter or design should be the focal point of your rug, not the fancy stitches.

If you can find no place for a fancy stitch in the body of your rug design, perhaps a textured border could be used. As some picture frames have texture, so can rug borders, a band of a repeated fancy stitch can really perk up an otherwise bland design.

## THE HALF CROSS STITCHES

The basic needlepoint stitch is the half cross stitch or, as it was once known, the tent stitch. It is called the half cross because it covers the intersection of two canvas threads just once. A cross stitch covers the same intersection twice but going in different directions each time. So you see, there is just HALF a cross stitch if one covers the intersection only once.

There are several ways of achieving this coverage in a half cross stitch but as far as rugs are concerned, the basket weave way is the best. Even though it puts more wool on the back of the canvas than the front, or so it seems, it is the best stitch to use because it distorts the canvas the least. If a canvas is badly pulled out of shape when it is worked, blocking will correct some of the bias but it will never be really right and true. Therefore, lack of distortion wins out over expense. Try to use the basket weave as much as possible, even in the subject matter of the design. Only the smallest details need to be worked in one of the other half crosses. The best one to use on mono-canvas is the continental stitch because the other one slips about on the mesh. If you are using a two thread canvas the simple half cross or quick-point can be used.

### THE BASKET WEAVE STITCH

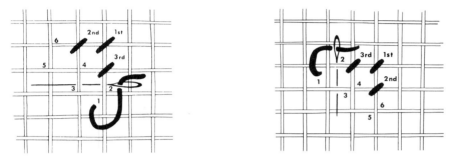

Remember that your needle always passes under two canvas threads. When you are working up from right to left, the needle is always going toward the hand holding the canvas. When you are working down from left to right the needle always points towards your body. A continental stitch at the end of the row will get you turned around.

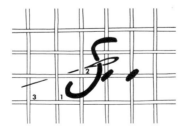

### THE CONTINENTAL STITCH

With the continental stitch the needle passes under two mesh and down one diagonally. Remember that the needle goes in the canvas back one mesh and up one mesh from where the wool is coming out. The stitch is worked from right to left and the canvas is turned around to start the next row. Before long you will have figured out how to do the stitch upside down and then you won't have to turn the canvas around any more.

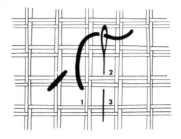

**THE HALF CROSS STITCH**
(only on two-thread canvas)

The simple half cross stitch or quick point stitch is simply twining the wool around and around one line of mesh using the needle as a bodkin. Working the stitch horizontally, one can stitch back and forth without turning the canvas around. The needle is pointing toward your body when the stitch is worked from left to right and away from you when worked right to left.

## THE BRICK STITCH

It is possible to work the brick stitch on both kinds of canvas, but it fits the mono-canvas best because it is an upright stitch. You may have to add more strands of wool to your needle to cover the canvas than you would use with the half cross stitch. It does not distort the canvas and it does not carry much wool on the back of the canvas. Worked in diagonal rows it is a very quick stitch. To work the half cross stitch next to it, one must cover every intersecting mesh as shown in the diagram.

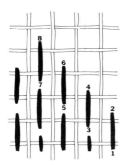

BRICK STITCH

BRICK STITCH COMBINED WITH
HALF CROSS STITCH

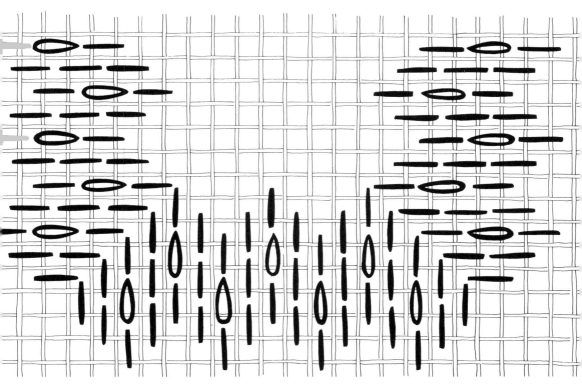

BRICK STITCH BORDER

## BARGELLO

Under heavy use, a stitch that covers several mesh is not going to wear as well as a shorter one. Therefore it would be better to use bargello for rugs that will receive a gentle amount of wear, such as a bedside rug. Wool behaves better on the canvas if it is coiled round and round rather than if it is bent or folded sharply. Stitches will lie

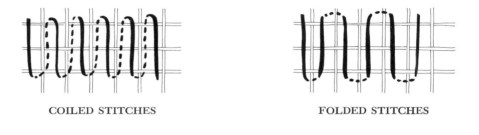

COILED STITCHES                    FOLDED STITCHES

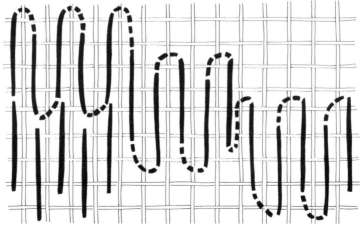

ECONOMY BARGELLO

flatter and not lean to one side. Many bargello patterns must be worked the coil way, which puts almost as much wool on the back of the canvas as the front. Diagrammed below is a way of working bargello so that it does not carry quite as much wool on the back, and still avoids folding the wool. Whichever way you start the stitch, the coiled way or the diagrammed way, continue that way for the rest of the rug. Otherwise a corduroy effect results which will never flatten out even after blocking. As with the brick stitch, more strands will be needed per needle to cover the canvas, and it is worked more satisfactorily on mono-canvas.

## THE KNIT STITCH

Rugs have been made completely of the knit stitch in Greece for years. They count two strokes of the stitch (forming a V) as one design unit, hooking them together to make a saw-toothed straight line or curved line.

### THE KNIT STITCH

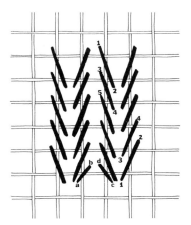

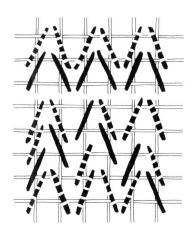

A. Lettered stitches are used to fill in at the end of a row.

B. Top line shows a straight outline, bottom shows diagonal outline.

A small knit stitch rug made in Greece, no other stitch is used. It is lined with burlap.

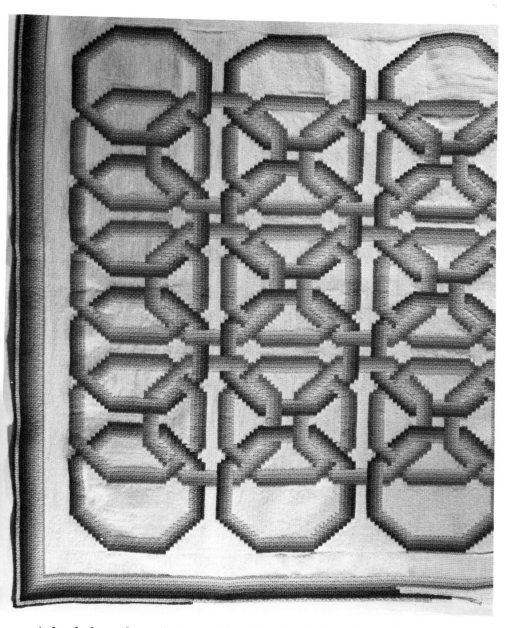

A detail of a six by six foot rug designed and worked by Mrs. Walter B. Smith of Washington, D. C. Mrs. Smith adapted the interlocking design from an illustration of a stone carving in an Islamic art book. The background is white and worked in knit stitch, the hexagons are in shades of blue-green, olive green, and gold, and are worked in rice stitch.

## THE SOUMAK STITCH

This stitch is a variation of the knit stitch, it goes under many names but since this is a rug book it should carry a rug weaving name. (In crewel work it is called the stem stitch.) The soumak stitch is just one half of the knitting stitch unit done over from two to four mesh. The more mesh one trys to cover per stitch the more wool one will need in the needle to cover the canvas adequately. Half stitches must be worked at the end of the row to fill in.

**SOUMAK STITCH**
The two mesh stitches fill in at the end of the row.

OPPOSITE. A detail from an 18th century Caucasian embroidery. The medallion shown is part of a pattern for a Kuba rug. The entire pattern is worked in stem stitch on blue and white gingham cloth. COURTESY OF THE TEXTILE MUSEUM WASHINGTON, D. C.

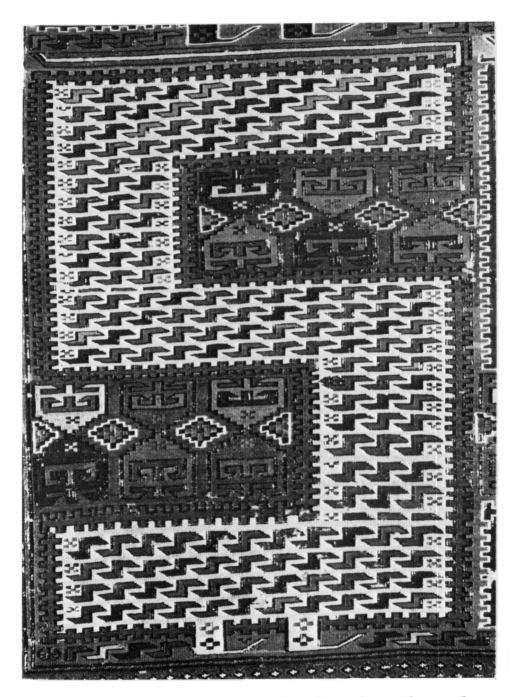

A detail from a Caucasian Soumak rug of the dragon design. This is a flat woven rug, though the effect is that of embroidery. COURTESY OF THE TEXTILE MUSEUM, WASHINGTON, D. C.

## THE MOSAIC STITCH

Worked square by square the mosaic stitch will distort the canvas quite a bit. If the small stitches are worked first, diagonally à la basket weave, and then the long strokes are filled in vertical or horizontal rows, the canvas will remain remarkably true. Working

**MOSAIC STITCH**

A. Short strokes first

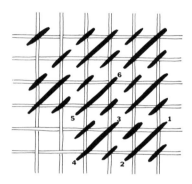

B. Long strokes last

C. Mosaic stitch variation

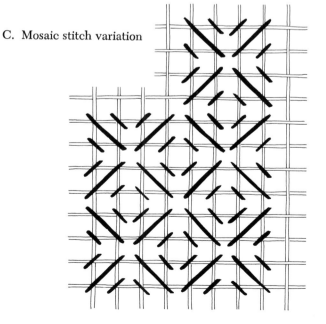

the stitch this way puts a fair amount of wool on the back of the canvas, but not any more than if the stitch is worked by the square. An interesting variation of the mosaic stitch can be achieved by working the squares in groups of four, with the long strokes pointing into the center; this gives the effect of a much larger stitch.

## THE DIAGONAL MOSAIC STITCH

This stitch can be worked in almost the same manner as the plain mosaic stitch and again with little or no distortion. Work the small stitches first diagonally and then, still working diagonally, fill in the long strokes.

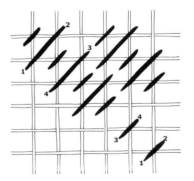

DIAGONAL MOSAIC STITCH
Short strokes first, long strokes last

## THE LEAF STITCH

This stitch can serve as the pattern of a rug by itself, or as a backgrounding or a border. An extra strand may be needed to cover

**A. THE LEAF STITCH**

On the left it is numbered the coil way,
on the right it is numbered the fold way.

B.  Leaf stitch border and corner

if you use the stitch on two thread canvas. The leaf stitch looks more even worked the coil way, but this puts as much wool on the back of the canvas as on the front.

C. Leaf stitch in stripes

Rosetta Larsen adapted from a black and white photograph this design from the St. Cyr convent in France for Mrs. Jack Desbecker of New York. PHOTO BY HELGA STUDIOS.

A cross stitch rug made in Pennsylvania in the 1870's on burlap, lined in plaid cotton. COURTESY OF D. G. RYPKA ANTIQUES, MIDDLEBURG, VIRGINIA, NOW OWNED BY THE YORK HISTORICAL SOCIETY, YORK, PENNSYLVANIA.

## THE CROSS STITCH

The time-honored needlepoint rug stitch is the cross stitch. Very popular in the nineteenth century, it is used less now perhaps because people don't like to cover the same ground twice. It is a very useful stitch for texture, borders and for working over joins. Be careful that the stitches all cross in the same direction.

**THE CROSS STITCH**

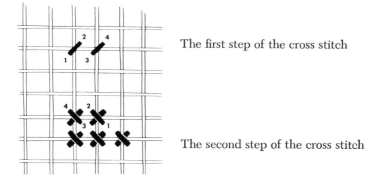

The first step of the cross stitch

The second step of the cross stitch

## THE SMYRNA CROSS STITCH

Another old favorite rug stitch, the Smyrna cross stitch is also known by several other names. It has a bumpy popcorn texture which is rather pleasing for borders. The stitch also comes in handy to cover joins (see page 60).

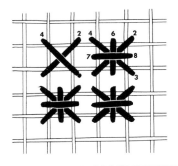

THE SMYRNA CROSS STITCH

## THE GREEK STITCH AND
## THE LONG-ARMED CROSS STITCH

The result on the front of the canvas looks the same for these two stitches, it is on the back of the canvas that the difference shows. They both start with a cross stitch. In Portugal a very beautiful type of rug called Arraiolos is worked exclusively in the Greek stitch on a special jute canvas. All the strokes of the stitch on the back of the canvas must be parallel for it to be a true Arraiolos rug.

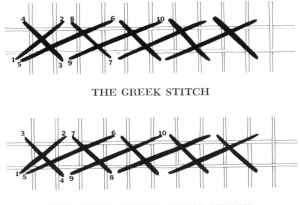

THE GREEK STITCH

THE LONG-ARMED CROSS STITCH

## THE DIAGONAL LONG-ARMED CROSS STITCH

Strangely enough this stitch combines better with the Greek stitch than with the straight long-armed cross stitch. All three stitches produce a firm surface on the face of the canvas and carry little wool on the back.

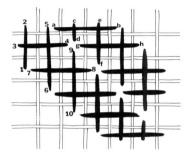

THE DIAGONAL LONG-ARMED CROSS STITCH

## THE HERRINGBONE FAMILY

There are four variations of the herringbone stitch, the strokes are always the same, the difference comes in the direction you work or how close you place the rows. All of the variations will work on both mono-canvas and two thread canvas.

The straight herringbone stitch gives a hard tight surface to a rug, but is hard to work unless the canvas and wool fit just right. One has to sort of peek up under the previous row of stitches to find the top mesh to stitch. Each row starts and finishes with a cross stitch. A cross stitch is worked in the spaces created in your first row of

ABOVE. A detail from the pictured Arraiolos rug showing how the outlining stitch is worked in a different direction than the background.

OPPOSITE. A modern Arraiolos rug from Portugal. COURTESY OF IBERIAN IMPORTS, ALEXANDRIA, VIRGINIA.

stitches and your last row, as shown in the diagram. This variation is worked from right to left only.

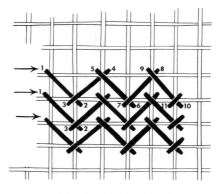

THE HERRINGBONE STITCH

The herringbone gone wrong or the reverse herringbone is the same stitch as the straight herringbone except that it is worked from right to left AND left to right. This creates a diagonal woven texture. It is a little easier to work than the straight version but still requires peeking occasionally under the previous row to find the mesh. Little one mesh cross stitches are again going to fill the every other mesh gaps produced at the top of the first row and the bottom of the last.

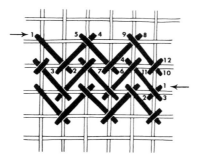

THE REVERSE HERRINGBONE STITCH

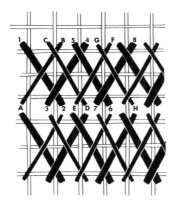

THE TWO-COLOR HERRINGBONE STITCH

The two color herringbone stitch forms a braid. One journey across the canvas is taken with one color of wool ricocheting from one row to the next. The thread is finished off and then the every other empty mesh are filled with a different color thread on the next journey. The stitch may be worked with the herringbone braids all running in the same direction or in opposite directions, as you wish.

The telescoped herringbone stitch forms a braid too, but it is a less loose-looking braid than the two color herringbone or even the Greek or long-armed cross stitch braids. This time both top and bottom mesh are worked on the same journey.

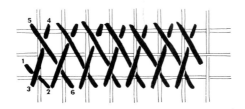

THE TELESCOPED HERRINGBONE STITCH

## THE LACED CHAIN STITCH

This is a very firm-feeling rug stitch with a honeycomb-like texture. There is not too much wool carried on the back of the canvas. The diagram shows how to add or subtract a stitch. The integral shape of the stitch at the edges must be preserved or the effect of

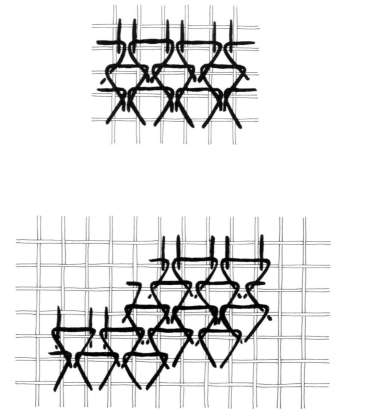

**THE LACE CHAIN STITCH**

the stitch is destroyed. To start the stitch, work a row of upright Gobelin stitches, two in every other set of mesh. On the next row pick up with your needle one Gobelin from each side to start the lacing. It helps to remember that the needle goes back in the hole from which it came, to complete each lacing or stitch. To fill in the little gaps left on your very first row of Gobelin and lacing, work two "half" Gobelin stitches per gap.

## THE DIAGONAL SHELL STITCH

The name of this stitch needs some explanation. When it is worked in horizontal rows it has a coil of wool added between each "sheaf of wheat". This must have resembled a shell to its inventor. The sheaf or shell stitch creates a bumpy thick surface with not too

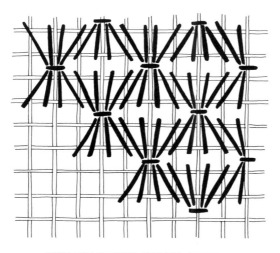

**THE DIAGONAL SHELL STITCH**
Note the half stitches on the right.

much wool on the back of the canvas. Being rough in texture, it is perhaps better suited to five mesh canvas than to a finer canvas. It may be worked in vertical rows or diagonal rows but it is easier to figure out worked vertically. If canvas shows between "sheafs" work a row of back stitches. One must peek under the upright stitches to make the horizontal stitch. The diagram shows how this stitch may be broken in half vertically and horizontally.

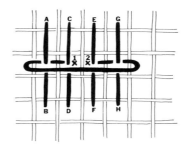

**THE DIAGONAL SHELL STITCH**

Stitch 1/2 is drawn tight, pulling the upright stitches into the sheaf shape. The upright stitches may also be worked the fold way.

## THE SURREY STITCH

This stitch produces a thick pile and is to be preferred over Turkey work if a denser pile is what you want. It has a slight tendency to slide about on mono-canvas but not enough to deter you from using it on that canvas. The stitch is worked from the bottom of the space up, as one does with Turkey work. The length of the pile will depend on what type of wool you will be using, three-quarters of an inch should be adequate for fine wools, and rug wool might call for an inch or more.

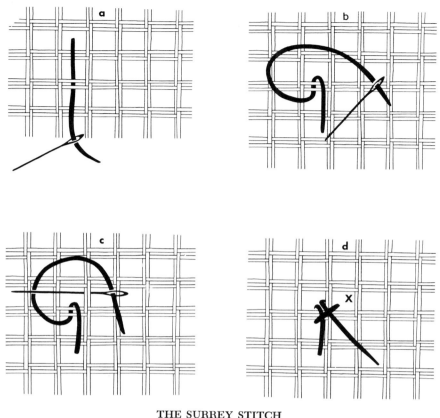

THE SURREY STITCH

To start the stitch bring the needle in and out of the canvas as in diagram a. Holding down with your thumb the tag of wool left out, bring the needle and wool around to the left. Insert it from the right in the hole next door as in diagrams b and c. The needle must pass over its own tail, so to speak, to form the knot. It is the same type of knot as the Turkey knot, the difference is that the surrey knot is worked at two angles. To start the next stitch insert the needle at X as in diagram d. To start the next row begin on the row of mesh just above the row completed.

## *TURKEY WORK*

Used for cushions and rugs, Turkey work was a popular seventeenth century stitch in Europe. Used today on rug canvas with rug wool it is a quick, fun stitch to do. It does not make a very dense pile if worked on mono-canvas with Persian wool, the surrey stitch fits this canvas better. Turkey work makes a very nice fringe on the edge of rugs (see Chapter Seven on Finishing Rugs). The stitch is worked from the bottom of your space up the canvas, it can be worked in either direction, left or right.

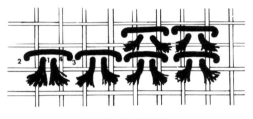

**TURKEY WORK**

# 4. Rug Joins

IT IS VERY difficult to make a join in a needlepoint rug that does not show slightly. This is a good thing to keep in mind while planning the design and layout of your rug. There is a basic conflict in rug making: if you want to carry small pieces with you to stitch wherever you may be, your rug will require many joins: if your pieces are large and less portable, your rug will have fewer joins. You must make your mind up as to whether you want "portability" or "joinability".

The easiest rug to make is a one strip rug, a forty-inch-wide

piece of canvas selvedge to selvedge, and then as long as you like. To prepare the canvas for working, fold back along one line of mesh hems of an inch and a half on the cut ends of the canvas. Baste them in place with carpet thread. Work your needlepoint through both layers of mesh, leaving one row of mesh at the fold unstitched. Work your stitch on the sides right to the selvedges. Treat the other end of the canvas the same way. When the needlepoint is finished, work either the binding stitch or the buttonhole stitch over the selvedges and along the folded ends. You might prefer to fringe the folded ends. Directions for the stitches will be found on pages 90 and 91 and for the fringe on pages 92 and 93. If you want to make a small rug, the folded edges could become the sides, and the selvedge the ends. Another way to make a small one piece rug is to turn back hems on all four sides when the needlepoint is finished. The four corners are mitered and the hems blind-stitched flat. The rug may be lined or not.

Fold the corner of the canvas back towards the center of the canvas. Cut the tip of the corner off to within a half-inch of the nearest wool stitch. Fold the sides down so that a short diagonal seam is formed which you will whip-stitch with carpet thread.

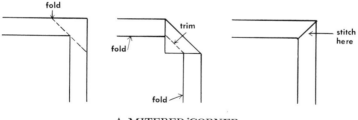

A MITERED CORNER

OPPOSITE. A strip rug designed and worked by Mrs. Sims Garret of Marietta, Georgia. Mrs. Garret used scrap wool left over from other needlepoint projects. PHOTOGRAPH BY HELGA STUDIO.

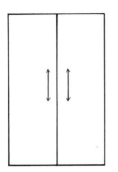

Fig. 1 Seamed,
layered over woven,
reinforced with strip

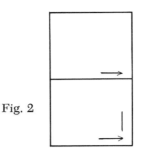

Fig. 2

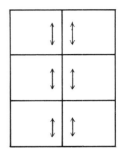

Fig. 3 Seamed
throughout or three
woven and the strips
seamed

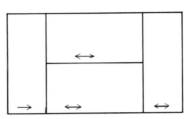

Fig. 4 Center, reinforced strip
or woven, ends seamed or layered
over

LAYOUTS WITH JOIN SUGGESTIONS
Arrows indicate direction of warp.

## JOINING TWO PIECES OF CANVAS

The next easiest way to make a rug is to work it in two long strips (figure 1) or in two fairly large squares (figure 2). These strips may be joined in various ways, some of which depend on the kind of canvas you are using. The least complicated method is just to sew the two pieces as you would a seam, matching mesh for mesh as you sew. (If you have a sewing machine which will take heavy fabrics, a line of stitching about a third of an inch from your needlework will help keep mono-canvas together. After your join is completed, the excess canvas is trimmed away and this will prevent ravelling.)

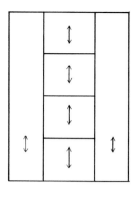

Fig. 5  Woven center or seamed,
strips seamed or layered over

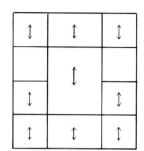

Fig. 6  Woven or seamed
border, center layered over

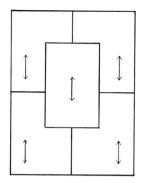

Fig. 7  Seamed

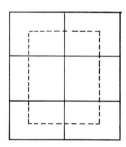

Fig. 8  Border design
does not have to
conform to seams

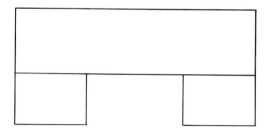

Fig. 9  Hearth rug, seams woven, seamed or
laid over

To plan this kind of join, you have only to leave the usual one and a half or two inches of excess canvas border. Work the pieces completely and then back stitch them together working through the last row of worked stitches. Work to the very edges of the canvas. If you have access to weaving supplies, try linen warp thread (2-ply) or use stout carpet thread. When the seam is finished, lay open the

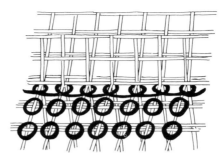

Joining two pieces of canvas, the seam sewn
in the last row of worked stitches

seam allowance. Some people like to sew a strip of twill tape over the seam as extra insurance. This will add extra bulk to the joint and seems like wasted effort. Blind-stitch the excess canvas seam allowance to the backs of nearby stitches and miter the corners. When you come to the join, snip out the excess canvas next to the seam to within a half inch of the work.

A variation of this join which works particularly well with two thread canvases is to back-stitch a seam between the two threads of the next set of mesh to your completed needlepoint. When the rug is turned to the right side you will see that a new two thread set of mesh has been created. This will be covered with the appropriate

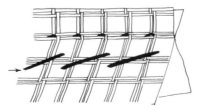

Joining two-thread canvas, forming a new mesh

colors of wool to conform to the pattern in a half cross or a cross stitch. Using this join with mono-canvas, one must work from the front of the finished canvas and whip-stitch or lash the canvas threads nearest the work. This will form one rather thick new canvas thread. Cover this with your wool stitches. To plan for this kind of join, you must not work one row of your pattern on either one piece or the other, it doesn't matter which.

Still another variation is to leave two mesh deep unworked on either side of your proposed join. Sew the two pieces of canvas together forming another mesh. Now there are five rows of mesh unworked. Work your needlepoint stitches over the five bare rows

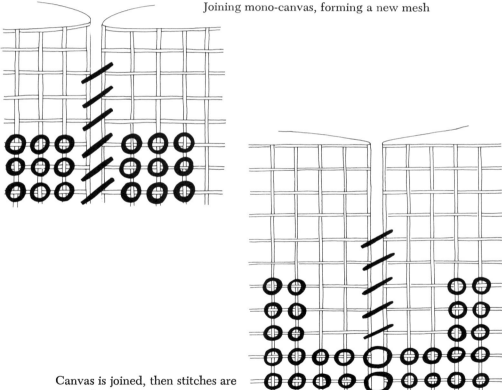

Joining mono-canvas, forming a new mesh

Canvas is joined, then stitches are worked over five-mesh strip.

ABOVE. About a dozen friends of Mr. Edmund N. Carpenter, Jr., of Wilmington, Delaware, joined together to make this charming rug as a wedding present for him and his bride. Each floral square is initialed by the worker. Note how well perspective is achieved in the house in the center. COURTESY OF MR. EDMUND N. CARPENTER, JR., PHOTO BY WILLARD STEWART.

OPPOSITE. A small hall runner was made by applying a needlepoint border to a strip of wool carpeting. The canvas was five mesh, the wool was rug wool. To make the border fit smoothly down the sides, it must be worked a few inches on first one side and then the other.

the length of the rug. The canvas mesh of the excess canvas in the back of the rug should be matched with the mesh on the face of the canvas so that it is just as though you were working on only one thickness. This makes a very secure join. If your design is at all elaborate this join would be tedious to do, working the design and the different color wools into the join as you would have to do.

Except for the straight back-stitch seam, most joins involve working through two or three layers of canvas. These layers add thickness to the seam, but if the rug is interlined or if it is laid on a soft rug pad this will be no problem. The following join has three layers of canvas and is usable for any of the larger mesh two thread canvases. It involves the use of liquid latex or Rug-Sta painted on the edge of the canvas to prevent ravelling.

First cut a strip of canvas eight mesh wide and as long plus hems as your seam is to be. Paint the outside mesh with latex all around the strip. Then paint the outside mesh of your rug lengths. They will be dry in a few hours. Only four pattern mesh on each length need be dedicated to the join. Two mesh per length will be needed to turn back, the fold will be made between the mesh rather than on the mesh. The total mesh involved will be six to the cut latexed edge. To make the join, fold the two mesh back on the length and with carpet thread baste it to the long strip four mesh in. Baste the other length to the strip after folding back the two mesh, and cover the remaining four mesh on the strip. Match mesh for mesh so that it will be as if you were working over just one thickness of canvas. Now work your needlepoint stitches across the eight mesh the length of the canvas, changing your color as you go. When the needlework is completed you will notice that when the rug is flat on the floor the join hardly shows at all, but if you fold the rug near the join a crack will show. Because of the nature of the weave and thread in mono-canvas this join will not work. It shows a large crack even when the rug lies flat. Whip-stitch the excess canvas hem together at each end, and trim the strips' excess canvas

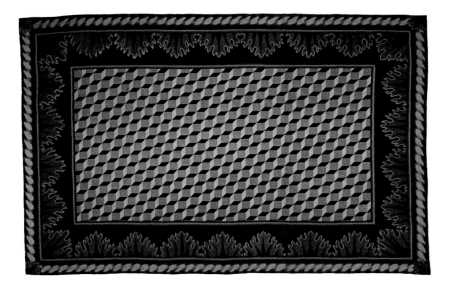

An interesting design combines a wavy border with a geometrical center.
Designed and worked by Louis P. Gartner, Jr.

A geometric design created by Mrs. J. Alton Boyer of Washington, D. C., and
worked by Mrs. Boyer and her sister, Mrs. Robin Henry of New York. The rug
is worked in the Smyrna cross stitch, the rice stitch and bargello. It was worked
in two large square pieces, the join is slightly off center. Seven mesh penelope
canvas and Persian yarn were used.

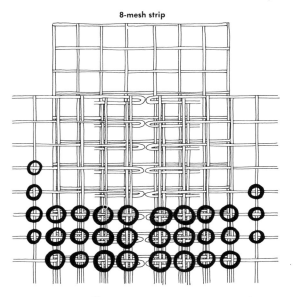

Two-thread canvas strip join. Shown on mono-canvas to make a simpler diagram

right back to the body of the rug. Hem back the canvas, miter the corners and finish the edges as you wish.

On any of the joins that involve working stitches over the seam, be sure you work the join stitches in the same direction as the worked rug stitches. The difference in direction will show, especially if the rug has been worked in quick-point.

A very simple two layer join can be accomplished by simply laying one cut edge of canvas over the other and then working through both. Plan on four bare mesh to the cut edge on each piece. Overlap three mesh over three, there will be a single mesh, single thickness, on each side of the overlapping. Therefore, a total of five mesh will be allotted to the join in your design. This is a somewhat risky join to make without first very neatly latexing the cut edge outside mesh. The danger is that the canvas will ravel as you are working it. Using the half cross stitch, it works well on the two thread canvases but on mono-canvas, even after latexing, the last thread of canvas on the cut edge will pull free if any heavy stress is applied. However, working a row of Smyrna cross stitch or the binding stitch (worked flat over two mesh) over the cut edge hides it nicely. The tufts of turkey work will also hide the cut edges. A small piece of cloth should be patched over the cut edge of the excess canvas when it is turned back and hemmed to prevent its ravelling.

A more indestructible way of working this join is to fold the cut edge back two mesh and lay it over the other piece of canvas three mesh in. Baste with carpet thread to match up the three layers of canvas. Five rows of the design would again be needed for the join, three on the folded side and two on the receiving side. Before you fold the cut edge back, there would be five mesh and on the receiving side there would also be five mesh. This join seems best

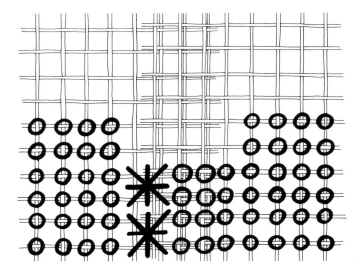

Cut edge laid over cut edge with Smyrna cross stitch covering the edge

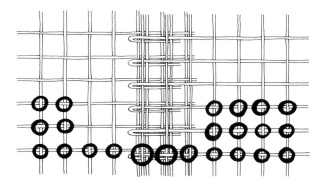

A fold-back of two-mesh laid three-mesh in from the needlework

suited for the two-thread canvases and should not be attempted with mono-canvas unless the cut edge is latexed first. The result will be lumpy but again the Smyrna cross stitch helps.

If you are willing to invest a considerable amount of time to the joining of your rug and wish to have a very secure and reasonably well hidden join, try the woven one. It works best for the two thread canvases, a slight ridge shows when mono-canvas is used. The following instructions apply to the two thread canvas, a different technique is used for mono-canvas.

You will need four inches of bare canvas on one of your pieces to be joined and just an inch and a half on the other. When the rug is worked, ravel the canvas back on the four inch piece to within four sets of mesh away from the completed needlework. Lay the ravelled piece over the other piece so that there are two sets of mesh showing on the other piece through the ravelled threads. You will be working through two layers of canvas for four mesh and the ravellings will be woven into the last two rows of mesh on the bottom piece. Baste the two pieces together, mesh over mesh. Then thread a large-eyed needle with a pair of mesh threads and weave them be-

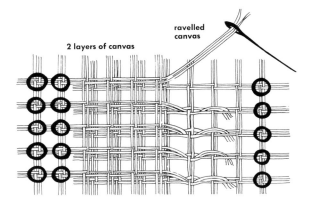

Stitches worked over both layers of canvas and over the woven-in canvas

tween the two threads of the mesh on the other canvas. If the other set of mesh threads spread, just poke them together again with the needle. Pull the threads through to the back and repeat the process the length of the join. Work about an inch out into the excess canvas border. When the weaving is finished, you will work your needle-point stitches over the two layers of canvas and over the double woven mesh. Trim the fringe of canvas threads poking out the back of the canvas to within about half an inch of the rug. The excess canvas hem may be turned back as usual. Since it is woven it will not spread.

If you want to try this method on mono-canvas you will have to wind or twine the ravelled threads around one by one rather than weaving by pairs. They all must be wound in the same direction and pulled from the back occasionally to keep them tight as you work. A trial run on a piece of canvas similar to the type you plan to use would be recommended to make sure you will be satisfied with the result.

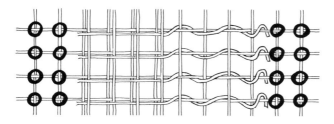

Ravelled mono-canvas threads wound rather than woven

## JOINING FOUR PIECES OF CANVAS

The very simplest way to join four pieces of two thread canvas is the cut edge over cut edge way. If you are using a highly sized five mesh canvas, latexing the very outside mesh is not necessary; it becomes more of a necessity if you are using seven mesh or ten mesh per inch canvas. Join a pair of the four pieces by laying three

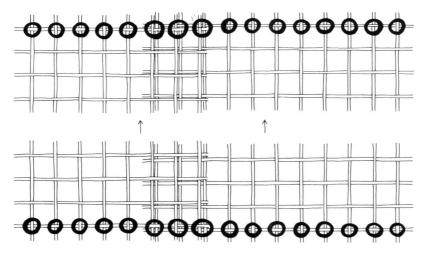

The bottom pair would be laid over the top pair and matched by mesh.

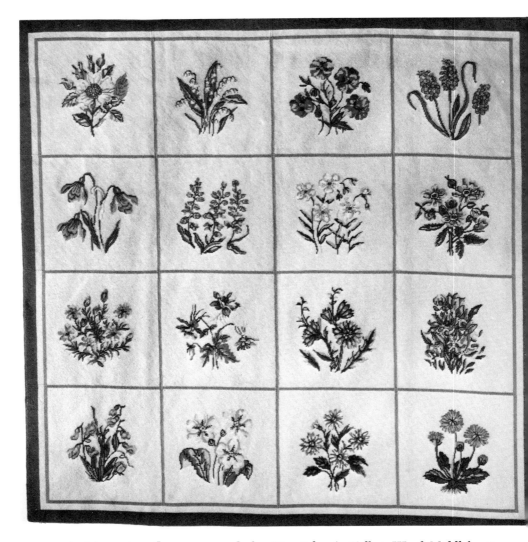

A sixteen-piece flower rug made by Mrs. John A. Talbot III of Middleburg, Virginia. Note that the outside borders are wider than the inside borders on the outside pieces.

mesh over three mesh and working through both layers with whatever stitch you are doing or with the Smyrna cross stitch. Work your
stitches to within three mesh of the next side to be joined. Join the
other pair of pieces the same way. Now lay one pair over the three
mesh of the other pair and stitch through again, matching the mesh
so that it appears that you are working through just one layer. Sometimes canvas thread ends will peek through when only the half cross
stitch is used. Cross stitches with the top stroke worked in the same
direction as the half cross stitch will help hide them. Cloth patches
should be stitched over the cut edges of the excess canvas to keep
it from coming apart. Painting lightly with latex will hold it in place
also.

There are only two ways to seam four pieces of canvas together,
and the second is a variation of the first. Neither method is easy to
do well the first time, for some reason or other. The first way is to
back-stitch the pieces together using the first row of mesh already
occupied by needlepoint stitches. The stitches must be tight, firm
and match mesh for mesh. When you have joined the four pieces
together work a cross stitch of wool through the point of each corner

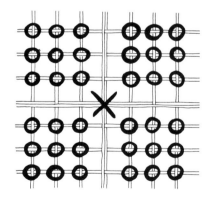

Four pieces seamed together with a cross
stitch at the center of the join

from the back. Work from one corner to the catty-corner, taking the needle through nearby excess canvas mesh to carry it on to its next corner. The reason for this cross stitch is to try to avoid a tiny hole at the center of the joining. Miter all four corners of each piece of canvas, this will make the corner square up neatly.

The other method of joining four pieces of canvas creates an extra mesh in the process. If you are using mono-canvas, whip-stitch the pieces together using the first empty mesh next to your needlepoint on each piece, as one does for two piece seams. Make a tight little cross stitch with carpet thread over the spot where the four pieces meet. Then using wool cover the line of mesh formed by the seam with the half cross stitch. When you come to the center of each

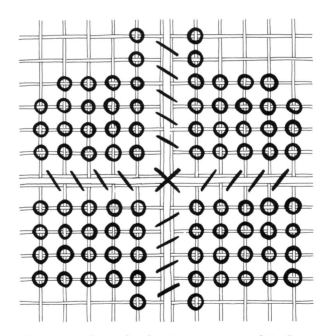

Four pieces seamed together forming an extra mesh in the process

join make a cross stitch over the carpet thread one to cover it completely. Make sure the top stroke is worked in the same direction as the rest. When all the pieces are joined, miter all four corners of the excess canvas on each piece.

On two thread canvases back-stitch up the middle of the set of mesh nearest the needlework. When all four pieces have been joined you will see that one mesh has been forced up into the middle of the join from each of the four pieces. Lash these mesh together with a carpet thread cross stitch and cover it with wool as you cover the rest of the created mesh. Make sure your half cross stitches and cross stitches all are worked in the same direction.

## ADDING A CENTER TO A BORDER

A center piece of needlepoint may be attached to its border by laying it in place and stitching through the two layers as has been done in previous joins. As usual, this will work well for two thread canvas but less well for mono-canvas unless the join is covered with a bulky cross stitch. Especially with the finer meshed canvases, latexing the very outside edge of the center piece is a must. Cut the border pieces on the inside edges to within five or six mesh of the work. The center piece should be cut to three mesh away from the work and then delicately latexed. Lay the center piece over the border piece so that one bare mesh of border shows all around. Baste into place. As you can see, you will have four rows of mesh all the way around to cover with your wool stitching. If your border pieces needed joining it is assumed that you have already done this.

You do not have to use the same join throughout the rug if you can devise a combination which will fit your purposes. Diagonal border seam joins have not been included in this listing because they have a tendency to stretch and bulge. This is particularly true if the rug you make turns out to be a wall hanging because it is too beau-

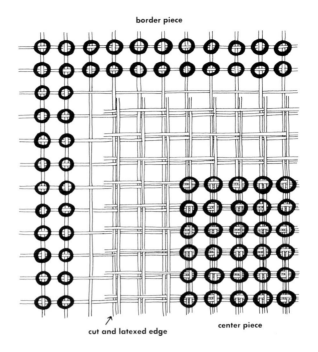

tiful to be walked on by mere mortals. A wall hanging diagonal seam is apt to stretch even if you cover the seam with tape to strengthen it.

## HEXAGONAL CORNERS

The only problem to cope with in making a forty-five degree angle corner is the saw-tooth edge on the right-hand angle if the half cross stitch is used. This can be cured easily by working a row of cross stitch on the edge row of stitches, slanting the top stroke in the same direction as the half cross stitches.

## CURVED EDGES

When you are designing a round or oval rug you must plan on losing one or two rows of stitches to the hem. Work your needlework as closely as you can to the curved line you have drawn on your canvas. Sometimes it will look very jagged and uncurving but when you come to hemming it back the curve will be quite apparent. Details for making a curved hem will be found in the chapter on finishing.

# 5. Putting the Design on the Canvas

SOME people prefer to work their needlepoint from graph paper designs and if you are doing a repeat pattern this is probably the most efficient way to work. Paper with ten squares per inch will do for simple repeats. A more elaborate design will require large sheets bought from an office stationer. Each square of the graph paper represents an intersection of two threads on the canvas. You will be counting squares on the paper and intersections on the canvas.

Needlepoint designing has one distinctive problem, since making a single line of half cross stitches from bottom right to the left

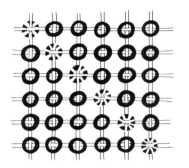

Dot-dot effect when working a single diagonal
line from bottom right up to the left

results in a dot-dot-dot effect. Making a single line from bottom left
to the right is simple because it follows the direction of the half
cross stitch. There are three ways of handling the dot-dots. Make
the thin line one mesh wider, which will give you a slightly zigzag
line, or work the surrounding stitches over the line completely and
later back-stitch the line in on top. The best method is to go ahead
and design single lines to the left and then cross stitch them, not
half cross stitch them. You will be surprised how few people will
notice.

Sketch your design out on the graph paper and then square it
off square by square. You will be making your decisions now on the
paper as to whether a square will be a background stitch or a subject
stitch. This facilitates the counting off when you are actually stitching
on the canvas. A good rule of thumb is that if the sketch line falls
in the square so that more than half is filled by the subject then that
square goes to the subject. If more than half is filled by background,
that square goes to the background. To actually start stitching, find
the center of the canvas by folding in quarters and marking the
center with a pin. Find the center of your design by the same method
and start stitching.

If you are quite satisfied with your sketched design and plan to paint your canvas, the next step is to enlarge the design to use as a cartoon. There are two ways of doing this. One is to have your sketch photo-stated. This is definitely not the cheapest way to do it but it is the easiest. Just tell the photographer how large you want the finished product to be. Obviously, he cannot enlarge to three feet by five feet for instance, on one print. However, a subject that large could be broken into segments for enlarging and then the prints could be joined with Scotch tape.

The other way of enlarging your design is the cross-hatching method, a do-it-yourself project. Cross-hatch your design (or lay a piece of tracing paper over it and cross-hatch that) into inch or half inch squares. Count the number of squares you have produced lengthwise and divide that number into the number of inches of the length of your planned rug. The idea is to transfer the design contents of each one of the small squares into a larger square, thus producing section by section your enlarged design. The result of your division above is the size of the square of cross-hatching you must draw next. For example, thirteen half inch squares divided into a desired thirty-nine inch length will result in three inch enlarged cross-hatchings.

If you are planning a large one-piece rug, an old door or a huge piece of wallboard will serve as a drawing board. You will need the largest layout or tracing paper tablet you can buy, or a wide roll of brown wrapping paper. Tape the layout paper together to make a large enough sheet. If you are making a large pieced rug, your paper and drawing board or table will have to match the size pieces of canvas you plan to work upon. Tack your paper to your drawing board and transfer the contents of each little square into its corresponding larger square. When the job is done, go over the whole design with a waterproof magic marker to make the lines dark enough to see through the canvas which will be laid over the cartoon.

When you buy your canvas make sure there are no knots in it.

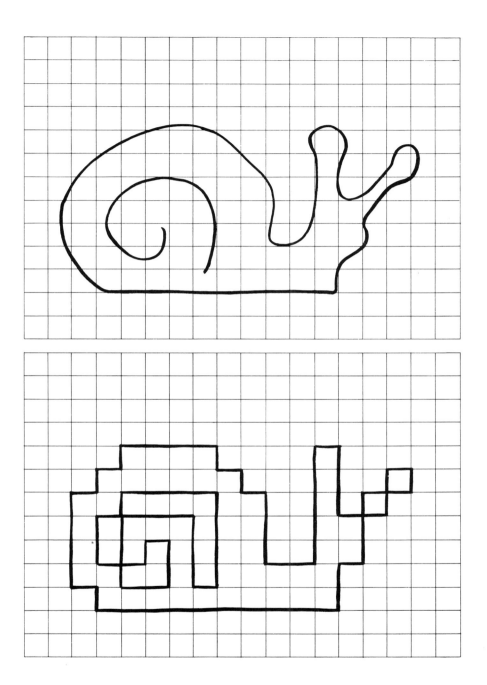

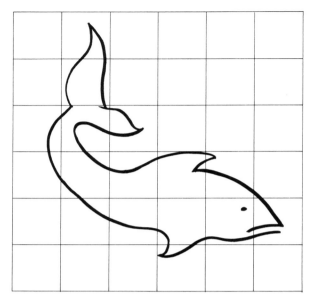

Enlarging a design by squares

This would be the weakest part of your rug, and since a rug really takes more wear than a pillow, a knot is a serious flaw. This may necessitate your taking from the needlework shop pieces of canvas rather than one long length (unless, of course, you are making a one-piece rug). Insist that you have a selvedge on each piece so that you can tell which way the warp goes, and that the pieces all come from the same roll of canvas. One of the most important things to remember in making a pieced rug is that the warp and weft must go in the same direction for each and every piece! Even though the canvas looks as if there were the same number of threads in the warp as in the weft, it isn't so. You will find that there are usually more weft threads than warp. (The warp threads are the ones running parallel to the selvedge.)

If you count out 140 threads weft-wise and then 140 threads warp-wise on ten mesh canvas, instead of a nice fourteen inch square, you will find that the measurements will be something like fourteen and a half inches on the weft and thirteen and seven-eighths on the warp. The importance of this to you in rug making is that unless all the pieces of the rug are cut so that the warp runs in the same direction, the pieces won't match and you will have to ease the pieces together, thereby giving a wavy join. It doesn't matter if the warp threads are right side up or not, just so the warps run parallel. You may find that sticking to the warp direction results in wasting canvas, so be it. As in dressmaking with a patterned material you might even need extra yardage.

Ideally, try to cut your pieces out of one length of canvas so that as they were in the canvas, so will they be on the floor. Diagram your pieces as you have them in the canvas on a piece of paper and number each piece. Then when you put them together you will have a map to go by. Dressmakers' chalk pencils or a crayon will do to draw cutting lines on the canvas. Before you cut, mark the top of each piece of canvas and the piece number in one corner border. With chalk or crayon, outline the working area and make any allowances you might need for the join. You might need an extra inch of canvas for an overlapping join, so try to "think through" each join now. If fancy stitches are to be used, check now to see if you need an odd or even number of mesh to accommodate them. Pieces that are to be joined together must have the same number of mesh; it is the mesh, not the inchage you must join, so double check! Unless the join dictates otherwise, leave a two inch or an inch and a half border around the working area on all sides. Some of this canvas will be cut away later but you will need it for blocking the piece when it is finished.

Cut the canvas evenly along one line of mesh. You may paint the cut edges with Rug-Sta (latex) a few mesh deep or bind them with inch wide bias tape. This will keep the canvas from ravelling as you work it. Tack your design cartoon to the drawing board. Lay the canvas over it. Line up the outside outline on the canvas with the outside outline of the cartoon. You will have to ease the canvas sometimes to make it conform to the outline. Tack it down and you are ready to paint!

If the design is very simple, crayons will do an adequate job. When you have finished coloring it in, lay paper towels over and under the canvas and go over the towel "sandwich" with a hot iron to take off some of the excess wax.

A more detailed design will require a paint job. The professional needlepoint designers use oil paints which they thin with turpentine to the consistency of cream. A few drops of Japan dryer added to the paint will hasten drying considerably, though it will very slightly darken the color.

Acrylic paints work very well for canvas painting, and are dry enough to stitch over in about four hours. Thin acrylics to the consistency of cream and mix a shade lighter than you really want, as they dry darker. There is still some professional hesitation about using acrylics as no one knows just what they will do to the canvas over a long period of time, but so far, there has been no problem.

Although magic markers are marked waterproof, many needlepointers have come to grief using them without first testing them on canvas. The reason that markers must be waterproof is because the canvas will be wet when it is blocked or later cleaned and the medium used should not run. AD Markers made by the Cooper Color Company of Butler, New Jersey, come the closest to filling the bill. They have over 120 colors to choose from, and a fat nib as well as a fine line. Magic markered canvases should be handled with

This rug design was adapted from the Eagle Gunpowder label used on the highest grade of gunpowder produced by du Pont in the 1850's. The rug was worked by the late Mrs. Lammot du Pont. COURTESY OF MR. WILLIS H. DU PONT.

The map of Fisher's Island was worked by the late Mrs. Lammot du Pont. The border depicts the summer pleasures of the island. COURTESY OF MR. WILLIS H. DU PONT. PHOTO BY BILL BLAKENEY, PALM BEACH, FLORIDA.

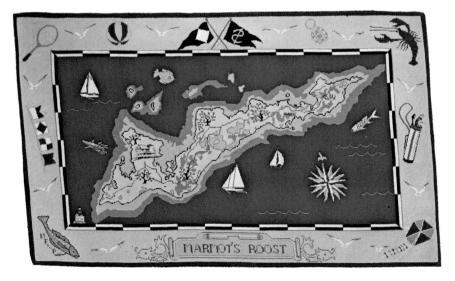

Alice Morgan Carson of Massachusetts designed the very masculine rug for
Mr. E. I. du Pont to work. It will be circular when its pine cone border is
finished. The animals are ones found in the Adirondacks. COURTESY OF MR. E. I.
DU PONT. PHOTO BY WILLARD STEWART.

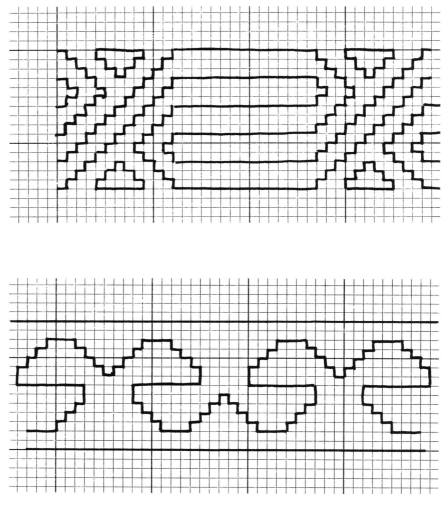

Graph designs for border motifs; they may be enlarged by drawing four squares for each one in the design. Each square represents a stitch.

good sense and care. Spraying with Scotch Guard is risky, as is wetting with Renuzit.

All of the above mediums will run somewhat if they become saturated with Scotch Guard or Renuzit. Oil paints and acrylics are waterproof after they become completely dry. Canvas with the most

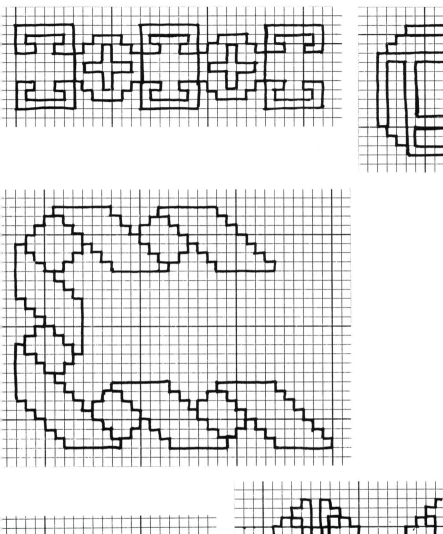
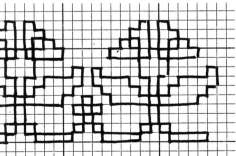
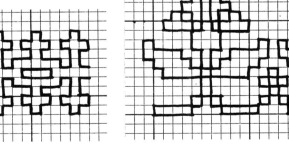

sizing is the easiest to paint on but will run when it is wet. Acrylics or oils only should be used on this type canvas, and to be super safe, spray the painted canvas with Blair Spray Clear Protective Coating after the paint is dry. Liquitex Gloss Polymer Medium may be brushed on when the paint is dry, or if you are using acrylics it may be mixed in with the paints. Canvas without much sizing sometimes acts like a wick when painted. To correct this, the Blair spray or polymer gloss should be used before you paint.

Your outlined design cartoon should shine through the canvas fairly clearly so that you can trace it out and color in. Some people are tempted to just trace the outline in one color throughout and then add the specific colors in wool as they work. This will work if the outline color is light enough. If a light color wool is worked over a dark color outline, the outline will "shine" through the wool.

A really well-painted canvas will have but one color per inter-section of canvas threads. If you have two colors in the same inter-section of mesh, when you are ready to stitch over that intersection you won't know which color to use. Try to think out the stitching as you paint—is the design helped by giving this intersection to the background or to the subject? If you can see that the paint is soaking through to the cartoon, the paint is too thin. Not much of the design should show in the back of the canvas if the consistency of the paint is just right. If, on the other hand, the paint is clogging the mesh, it is too thick. When you come to the second canvas, you may want to do some counting of mesh if your design carries from piece to piece to make sure the crossing lines register.

## FRAMES

A needlework frame is a great help in rug making if you know that you work rather tightly. A badly distorted canvas is never really going to come true again because it can't. The wool threads are firmly holding the canvas in the slanted position. A frame will hold

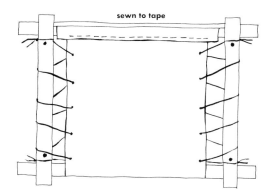

sewn to tape

Lashed canvas in frame; it must be re-lashed as
the work progresses and is rolled on the frame.

the canvas quite straight for you. The disadvantage of a frame to
some needlepointers is that you must stitch two-handed, one hand
on top of the framed needlework and the other underneath. You will
notice, however, that if you work this way the stitches will be much
more even in texture and your work will have a more professional
look. Needlepoint frames work on the scroll principle, the canvas is
pinned with upholsterers' pins or sewn to the tapes attached to the
long bars. The long bars are then turned to roll the canvas along,
tightening screws hold the bars in place. Lashing the free sides to
the short bars with carpet thread will make a more taut surface.

Your choice of frame is governed by the width of the rug pieces
you plan to work. Floor frames are available in forty and thirty inch
widths, hand frames may be had down to a foot in width. If you
have one large piece of canvas and don't want to use a scroll frame,
use one half of a large circular embroidery hoop. With carpet thread
lash the canvas firmly all the way around the hoop with the working
surface on top. When that area is worked, relash in the next spot.
If you have a small quilting frame, old or new, this will work as an

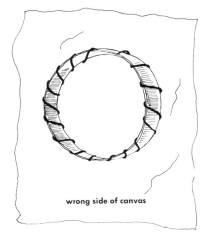

wrong side of canvas

A hoop frame lashed with carpet thread to the wrong side of the canvas. Turn it over to work. The hoop must be re-lashed in a new location.

embroidery frame. Even a pair of one by four or two by four boards laid over the backs of two chairs will do.

When you start stitching, be sure the beginning tags of each strand of wool are well secured. The heavy wear that a rug endures will work short tags loose and they will pop to the surface. Make a conscious effort to entrap the tag as you work. To finish off a strand, surface the end of the strand about an inch away from your last stitches and in the path of your oncoming stitches. Again make a conscious effort to ensnare the tag stretched out on the back of the canvas. When you feel you have ensnared it enough, just pull the surface tag through to the back and snip it off close to the canvas. You will find that finishing off this way will give a less lumpy look to your work, lumps formerly caused by running the tags through the backs of neighboring stitches. Of course, some stitches just don't have enough on the back of the canvas to hold down a tag and you have to weave them in.

If you plan to do the basket weave half cross stitch for the backgrounding, always mark the direction in which you were going when

you stop stitching. This will prevent those odd streaks one sees sometimes in a field of half cross stitch. The streaks are caused by working
a row in one direction, say right to left, followed by another row of
right to left, thereby repeating the direction of the last worked row.

It is thought by some that it makes a difference in the look of
your work if the wool threads are all worked in the direction in
which they are spun. This is a moot point. If you wish to experiment,
cut your next skein of wool in two places, pick up the left end of
one of the halves and lay it beside the right end of the other half,
now all the threads are going in one direction. Run your fingers
along one thread. If the thread bristles slightly under your tender
touch, you are working against the spin. Try the other direction and
your fingers will run smoothly. Tie a thread near one end of the cut
skein so that you can consistently thread your needle from that end.
Compare when you are finished with a random-threaded piece.

Your darkest colors should be worked last because all wools
lose some fibers as they are handled. Dragging light wools over
worked dark wools will pick up some of these fibers and then they
will get themselves worked into the stitches. They are the very devil
to pick out when once worked in.

If you use the half cross stitch on a pieced rug, work a whole
cross stitch in each corner, the top stroke worked in the same direction as the others. This will give the corners a more covered look
when it comes to joining them.

# 6. Blocking Your Rug

EVERY rug needs some blocking no matter how expertly you stitch, if only to persuade each beautiful stitch to flatten out and look like the rest of the army of stitches. The least blocking you can get away with is to lay the rug or rug pieces face down on a clean surface (old clean window shades are wonderful for this purpose) and press away with an iron and damp pressing cloth. Tug here and there if the corners need shaping or wherever needed. Leave the rug for about twelve hours to dry completely.

OPPOSITE. A Norwegian design repeat pattern rug worked by Doctor Earle Silber of Chevy Chase, Maryland. It is a single strip rug, worked on rug canvas.

If your rug needs a little more blocking, you may have to tack it out and with the help of another person, dry stretch it into line. If you do not have an old door or an attic floor that you can sacrifice to your needlepoint, the next best thing to do is to buy a sheet of wall board or plyboard. Aluminum tracks are soft and will not go into hard woods, but they do not rust. Copper tacks corrode a little but they will go into hard woods. To avoid corrosion stains, stick a piece of masking tape down wherever you must tack. Architectural pins will hold the canvas in place on wall board as well as upholsterers' pins. Do not drive the tacks through the canvas threads, only through the holes. Some tacks are sharp enough to cut the canvas threads. Place the tacks about an inch from the stitching. After you have tugged the canvas into place and tacked it, go over it with the damp pressing cloth and the iron. A good steaming will moisten the sizing just enough hopefully to straighten any distortion.

If your rug is in several pieces, it is a good idea to outline in china marker on brown paper the exact size you want each piece to be after blocking. You will then have a guide to block to guaranteeing that all pieces will be uniform. Don't use a pencil for your outline

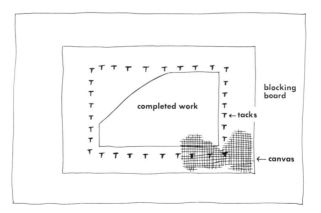

A curved rug section blocked

This abstract design rug in greens, yellows, browns, and red was made by a committee. The occasion was a needlework exhibition held at the Joslyn Museum of Art in Omaha, Nebraska, 1970. Thirty-five one foot square pieces were joined to make the five by seven foot rug which was auctioned off at the opening of the exhibition. The rug was designed by a member of the museum staff.

because it smudges and will dirty the face of your rug. Curved pieces should be treated as if they were square.

Many canvases need a more complete blocking than just steam pressing, with or without tacking. You will need an old sheet for the next method. Wet it and wring out as much water as you can by hand. Roll the rug in the wet sheet and pop it into a large plastic bag for four or five hours. Use one sheet per rug piece if you have any doubts about the color fastness of paint, wool or canvas. After sufficient time has passed, remove the rug from its swaddling clothes and laying it face down, tug and pull it into shape. Then tack it down, working evenly all around the canvas, first one side and the the other. If the pieces are large, you will probably need another person to help you. The advantage of the wet sheet method is that it loosens the sizing but does not carry it away as total immersion of the canvas does. However, if colors are going to run, they will just as much as if you had soaked the canvas.

The ultimate method is totally immersing the canvas. The main objection to doing this is the sheer size of the pieces you are blocking, as wet canvas and wool can be very unwieldy and not everyone has the kind of place to make and leave a mess. As mentioned before, the sizing often takes leave of the canvas when soaking and you are left with a mass of limp threads to try and join. The only reason one should resort to the total immersion of the canvas would be for a hopelessly distorted rug or rug piece. Really, no amount of blocking will help a tightly biased piece, it will look all right after blocking and then will quietly sneak back into its original shape.

Wet the rug completely in a set tub or bath tub, making sure it is really wet throughout. Remove from the water, soaking won't help, and wrap the rug in dry towels. Squeeze out as much water as you can. Then lay the rug face down on your blocking board. You might want to protect the board with a sheet of plastic or brown paper. Tug and tack the rug into shape. If you plan to size the canvas when the rug is dry now is the time to do it. Use either starch or a commercial sizing. Do not use rabbit skin on this type of needlepoint! It should be used just for purses and bookbindings.

After joining your pieces of rug together you will probably have to steam press over the joins, but further major blocking should not be necessary.

# 7. The Finishing Touches

HAVING stitched your rug, and then blocked it and joined it, the only things left to take care of are the hemming, the edging if you want one, and the lining. There are several ways to edge the rug: the binding stitch, button-holing, fringe and an applied edge. Depending on which edging you are going to use, if any, is the way the rug should hemmed. Directions for hemming will thus be included with the edging directions and the following are directions only for an unedged rug. It should be hemmed so that no bare canvas will show. If you used rug canvas, the hem should be folded back right on the last row of needlepoint and then firmly blind-stitched with carpet thread to the backs of stitches nearby. The corners should be mitered as you come to them. A finer meshed canvas should be folded back on the last two rows of work and then the hem is blind-stitched down. You may want to trim the canvas a little, but don't take off much, you'll need it if you ever wash and reblock. Flatten the edges and the corners with pressing cloth and iron and if you do not plan to line the rug you are finished!

The binding stitch is a practical as well as decorative finish. It could be compared to the serging put on carpets and some oriental rugs. It may be worked over one or two mesh of a pieced rug or over the selvedge of a one-piece strip rug. A pieced rug should be hemmed so that one or two mesh are showing at the edge, obviously no hemming is necessary on the selvedge. The binding stitch is always worked with the wrong side of the canvas facing you so that the braid formed will slant in the topmost direction. Fasten your wool in the backs of some nearby stitches. Run the needle through the first hole, bringing it through from the front side of the canvas to the back (even though the yarn is attached to the back). The needle always points toward you on this stitch. Work

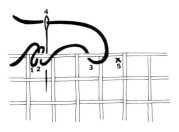

**THE BINDING STITCH**
The needle will make the fifth stroke at the X.

another stroke over the one just completed. Now skip one hole and make a long stroke over to the third hole. Go back to the first hole, then forward to the fourth hole which is the next available uncovered and unused hole, and so proceed up the canvas. Just remember that you always must skip one hole going in either direction. Going forward you always use the next vacant hole.

To finish and start a new thread, run your needle through the next hole and then down through some nearby stitches to lock the thread in. Run the new thread through the backs of nearby stitches and bring the needle out right at the hole where the spent thread came through on its last trip. Proceed to the next stroke. To finish off at the end, work the stitch down to the very last mesh. If there is canvas still showing, make a few little covering stitches, "fake it," as they say.

Instead of using the binding stitch one can use the buttonhole stitch over one or two mesh. The canvas should be hemmed in the way as for the binding stitch except that two or three mesh should be showing on the face of the rug. It will be over these mesh that the buttonholing should be worked. It makes a neat attractive finish to the edge of the rug. However, the edge takes a great amount of

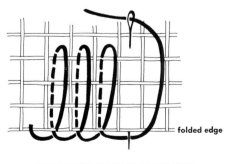

folded edge

THE BUTTONHOLE STITCH

wear, if one buttonholed stitch wears through, the edging will ravel quickly.

Fringe may be worked over a latexed cut edge or, if you prefer, over a folded hem. There are three ways of working it; woven, looped or knotted. The woven fringe must be worked one or two mesh extra on each side of the canvas, so it must be fringed first and then hemmed. For the other two ways, the rug may be hemmed and mitered, leaving one bare row of mesh at the fold.

To work the woven fringe, fold the canvas five or six mesh away from your last completed stitches. Baste-hem it so that the mesh match and it appears to be just one thickness of canvas, though you really have a double layer of five or six mesh. Or cut the canvas five or six mesh from the completed needlework and latex the cut edge. Using a file card as a gauge, stitch the fringe into place in the row of mesh closest to the needlework.

The fringe should extend at least two inches below the folded or cut edge of the canvas. Thread your needle with a contrasting shade of wool and weave in and out of the canvas, alternating mesh with each row. Try to keep your fringe (warp) threads neatly in line as you weave over them. Work to the very edge of

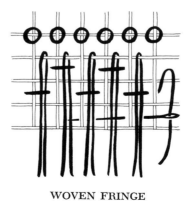

WOVEN FRINGE

the canvas or hem. Finish off your weaving threads by running them into the back of nearby stitching. When you are finished, trim your loops and hem back the side hems of the rug. Half-miter at the fringe corners.

Looped fringe can be worked with a crochet hook and the wool pre-cut. Five to six inch pieces should be long enough. Push the crochet hook through the empty mesh from the front and catch up a piece of pre-cut wool. Pull the wool loop through to the front and slip the dangling pieces from the back through the loop. Pull the dangling pieces tight.

A more adequately covering fringe would be achieved by working two rows of turkey work over the last row of completed needlepoint stitches and the following empty row of mesh. More than two rows of turkey work will stand up in a pile. A damp pressing cloth and a hot iron will persuade the two rows to lie flat. The fringe should be at least two inches long before trimming. (See page 48 for the Turkey work diagram.)

Conso rug tape makes a very neat bound edging for needle-point rugs but it is difficult to acquire. Carpet dealers have it but are usually loath to sell it by the yard retail. It comes in a great variety of colors. If you are lucky enough to get some, sew it face down to the very edge of your stitching which should be face up. Then

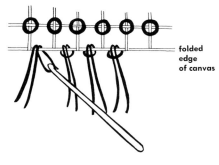

folded
edge
of canvas

**LOOPED FRINGE**

Antique American needlepoint rugs are rare. One of the few known examples is this one made by Anna Baker of Bakersfield, Vermont. It was made on linen with wool and measures 60 inches by 25 inches. The predominant colors are red, blue, yellow and brown. COURTESY OF SHELBURNE MUSEUM, INC., EINERS J. MENGIS, STAFF PHOTOGRAPHER.

turn the tape to the back of the rug and stitch it down, mitering the corners.

Rosetta Larsen of New York, the great lady of needlepoint, wraps cording with wool which matches the rug. She then blind-stitches the covered cording to the rug edge. She feels that it protects the edge of the rug from wear and is easier to replace than worn stitching. Miss Larsen sews small triangles of green rubber matting to the already lined corners of rugs to prevent skidding on hardwood floors.

Any even weave material may be used for rug lining. Linen works well as do homespun, denim, mattress ticking, burlap, or an even weave wool. Duck or canvas are best left to the professional finishers. They have the sewing machines strong enough to cope with such tightly woven and heavy materials. Pre-shrinking the lining is really not necessary unless you think the material will sag. Lay the rug face down on a large table or the floor and place the lining on top of it face down. The lining should extend about a half inch over the stitching all around the rug. If you had to seam lengths to make a large enough lining, be sure to trim away the selvedges. Using either upholsterer's pins or needle and thread, tack the lining to the rug here and there as though you were quilting it. This is to make sure that rug and lining are even throughout. Fold the edge of the lining under so that it just meets the edge of the rug stitching, prepared as described on page 89. Pin the lining to the rug, tucking the lining hem under as you work. Blind-stitch the lining to the edge of the stitching, picking up canvas and wool as the needle digs in. When the lining is attached, remove your pins or quilting tacks, and with iron and pressing cloth give it one final finishing pat.

An interlining would, of course, have been inserted before the lining. Burlap or a heavy weight pelon or an even weave woolen will do. Cut the interlining a third of an inch smaller than the rug stitching. Blind-tack the interlining to the needlepoint in scattered places and on the edges. It should have some anchors as it is apt to rumple up inside. Then the canvas hem is turned down and the lining attached. Mr. Robert Seibert of Seibert Decorators in Bethesda, Maryland, uses a fine latex spray, Scotch-Grip Spray Adhesive, number 44, to bond the interlining to needlepoint rugs. This means that the rug cannot be taken apart to wash and must always be cleaned. Incidently, Mr. Seibert cuts separate identical plywood forms for blocking rug pieces. The bare canvas is tacked to the sides of the form, the stitching just comes to the edge. This method guarantees that each piece will match up to its neighbor.

Hemming an oval rug is a very simple job. Because the stitching is uneven along the edge, to make the curve you will have to pull to the back about a quarter of an inch of stitching. As you pull you will notice that the excess canvas stretches or gives, making the curve all by itself. All you have to do is to stitch very securely about a third of an inch in from the fold, don't let the stitches show on the front, but stitch as permanently as you can. You should not have to make any little tucks if you pull the canvas enough so that it accommodates the curve. Trim the canvas to within three-quarters of an inch of the edge. If you can do so, latex the edge before you cover it with lining or a strip of bias cotton tape. The straight sides of the oval rug will have a couple of rows of stitching showing on the back too.

In the years to come your rug must receive reasonably gentle care. An occasional vacuuming with a hand machine or the brush attachment will pick up the obvious dirt. If your situation is such that you can give it a good shaking, that is even better than a vacuuming. If the rug is small enough to fit into the clothes dryer, and if you have a dryer that will run without the heat unit on, a five or ten minute tumble in the dryer will loosen a lot of grit and dust.

If the rug must be cleaned a gentle rug cleaner from the supermarket will do a very adequate job. Surface stains will come up with a spray product such as Goddard's spray cleaner or K2r. Dog accidents will clean up with a solution of one half a cup of ammonia to

This rug depicts six birds of Connecticut. The plain two-color border nicely sets off the bold design of the birds. COURTESY OF MRS. DONALD F. BUSH. PHOTO BY HELGA STUDIO.

a quart of warm water, if you can clean before the stain is twenty-four hours old. Pour a little clear warm water over the spot to rinse and then blot dry with paper towels, applying the pressure with your foot. If you must send your rug out to a commercial rug cleaner, really question him on the methods he will use, and the soaps. Particularly find out if a mechanical brush will be used on the surface, and if it will, find another cleaner for your rug.

Needlepoint rugs can be washed, but you must positively know whether the paints are waterproof and if any of the wools will run. The lining of the rug must be removed before washing. Use a mild soap such as Ivory Flakes in lukewarm water. Rinse thoroughly and then reblock the rug. When dry, reapply the lining.

# 8. Special Purpose Rugs

IN THE 1870's ladies' magazines were printing instructions on how to apply needlepoint borders to pieces of carpeting, animal skins and even turkish toweling. The idea of rug borders is worth reviving for stair carpeting or any other space where straight needlepoint might not be able to take the wear. The wool carpeting is where the hardest wear will be as the border winds its pretty way around the edge as decoration.

OPPOSITE. This well-worn bunny rug was worked by Mrs. Edith Pratt Maxwell and was cherished at boarding school by her granddaughters. COURTESY OF MRS. THOMAS P. DILLON.

The type of carpeting used is very important. Most synthetic carpeting and some woolen carpets have a rubber backing bonded to them or are heavily bundled with latex. This type of backing makes the carpet unsuitable for our purposes because it would be next to impossible to get a needle through it to sew the border on. A few of the top quality wool manufacturers such as Magee and Karistan make a wool carpeting with just a thin coat of latex on the back, thin enough for a needle to penetrate with relative ease. Rolls of carpeting are twelve feet wide. Unless your dealer is willing to cut it shorter, that is what you will be paying for. Too tall a pile on the carpeting looks strange with needlepoint. The taller the pile of the carpeting, the larger the mesh of the canvas must be to stay in proportion.

Select a canvas which will retain its sizing after blocking. Attaching a limp, spaghetti-like canvas to carpeting is a tedious job. You don't want the canvas to give an appearance of flimsiness next to the stiff carpeting.

A repeat design looks well on stair borders as does a trailing vine design. Motifs of significance to you and your family spaced evenly on a plain background look charming with any decor. It is a good idea to work your design out on graph paper so that you will know how many mesh are involved. You will need to know just where to place your motifs if they are separate ones so they will either land on the step or the riser. Measure your steps and risers, surprisingly you may find some variation. You may wish to have a design going across the riser of the first and last step, or you may just want side borders. Some thought should be given to the kind of join to be used. A woven join or a double thickness one is better than a sewn one. Sturdiness is important here. When you cut the canvas, remember to cut all the pieces in the same direction, either weft across, or up the warp. Depending on the kind of canvas you use, either the warp or the weft will stretch more than the other. If you cut all the pieces in the same direction, at least the stretch will be even. Leave a two- or three-inch excess canvas border on the carpet-

This woodland rug graces a bedroom in Blair House, the official guest house for distinguished visitors in Washington. It was made by a group of ladies from Ohio, Pennsylvania and Michigan expressly for the room in which it is used.
HOUSE AND GARDEN PHOTOGRAPH BY HORST.

This detail of a much larger rug shows part of the border. Everyone, even children, who worked on the rug had their initials included in the border. It was designed by Mazaltov of New York for Mrs. G. Burton Pearson, Jr. of Wilmington, Delaware. COURTESY OF MRS. G. BURTON PEARSON, JR., PHOTO BY WILLARD STEWART.

The left and right wings of the main altar rug at the National Cathedral, Washington, D. C. They were designed and mounted by the Misses Ruth, Marian, Elizabeth and Mary Tebbets of Kent, Connecticut.

ing side. This will be latexed to the carpeting later. After you have worked the pieces, try to block them in pairs. This also helps keep them even. If you are doing the weaving join, weave out into the excess canvas about one inch and into the corners, this adds strength to the join and makes the hem easier to do.

When all the pieces are all joined together, lay the border out on the floor to measure exactly the size carpeting you will need to go in the center. Cut the carpeting with a razor along one thread as you do with canvas. Trim any crusty latex selvedge, and any unevenness. Cut one long side of the carpeting and one short side. Place the carpeting in the border. You will need a curved upholstery needle and poly bond or carpet thread, two or three threads in a needle if you think you need them. Starting at the corner, go into a stitched mesh and then into the carpeting. If you have a riser piece, work across that and when you are certain of the measurements,

cut the other long side of carpeting. Sew first one side of the border and then the other, back and forth, to keep the sides even. Cut the bottom edge of the carpeting when you get there. If you feel the canvas needs more body, spray some starch on the back of the worked canvas. Spraying with a non-skid latex will glue the excess canvas border to the back of the carpeting and thus take some of the strain off the stitching holding them together.

Fold back the excess canvas on the outer edge and mitre the corners; if no further finishing is to be done on the edge, hem the canvas down. It is not necessary to line stair carpeting. Stair rods are the best way to secure your bordered carpet. If you must use tacks, try to use aluminum ones and if they bend too much, use copper. The copper corrosion will stain the carpet the least.

Some oriental rugs are flat woven, that is, they have no pile. There is a type of Turkoman flat woven rug that looks as if the design were embroidered on a plain tabby weave background. Actually the design has been woven in, superimposed, so to speak, on the basic warp and weft. It appears as if someone had not "filled in the background." Warp cloth makes a very good substitute for the Turkoman warp and weft. The dark reds and blues of the hand-dyed "embroidered" design can metamorphose into the fresh bright yarns popular today. One could brighten a beach house floor with such a rug, or cherish its softness as a bedside or nursery rug. If one were very ambitious, a bed rug could be made. Because warp cloth is so soft, one can work on fairly large pieces without feeling like Omar the tentmaker.

Warp cloth can be pieced or joined, but the join is rather obvious unless covered with big stitches. However, it comes in six-foot widths so piecing should not be too necessary. It is also available in more conventional widths. It is sold in rug hooking supply shops. The Heirloom Needlework Guild product has good body to it and a firm twist to its many-plyed thread, there are about thirteen or fourteen mesh to the inch. Persian yarn and some tapestry yarns will fit nicely. There is one drawback to warp cloth, the half cross stitch makes it bulge and hump. It is just right for bargello or any of the other long stitches such as the long armed cross stitch or the soumak stitch.

A conventional rug frame may be used or a large hoop frame. To prepare the cloth for working one should either machine-stitch around the usual two inch excess canvas border to prevent ravelling or one should bind with bias tape. Warp cloth is cut just as canvas is, along one thread. Crayons, in the colors you will use, work well to

OPPOSITE. A detail from a flat woven Turkoman rug showing the border and the center pattern. The plain tabby weave shows behind the dark red, blue and orange designs.

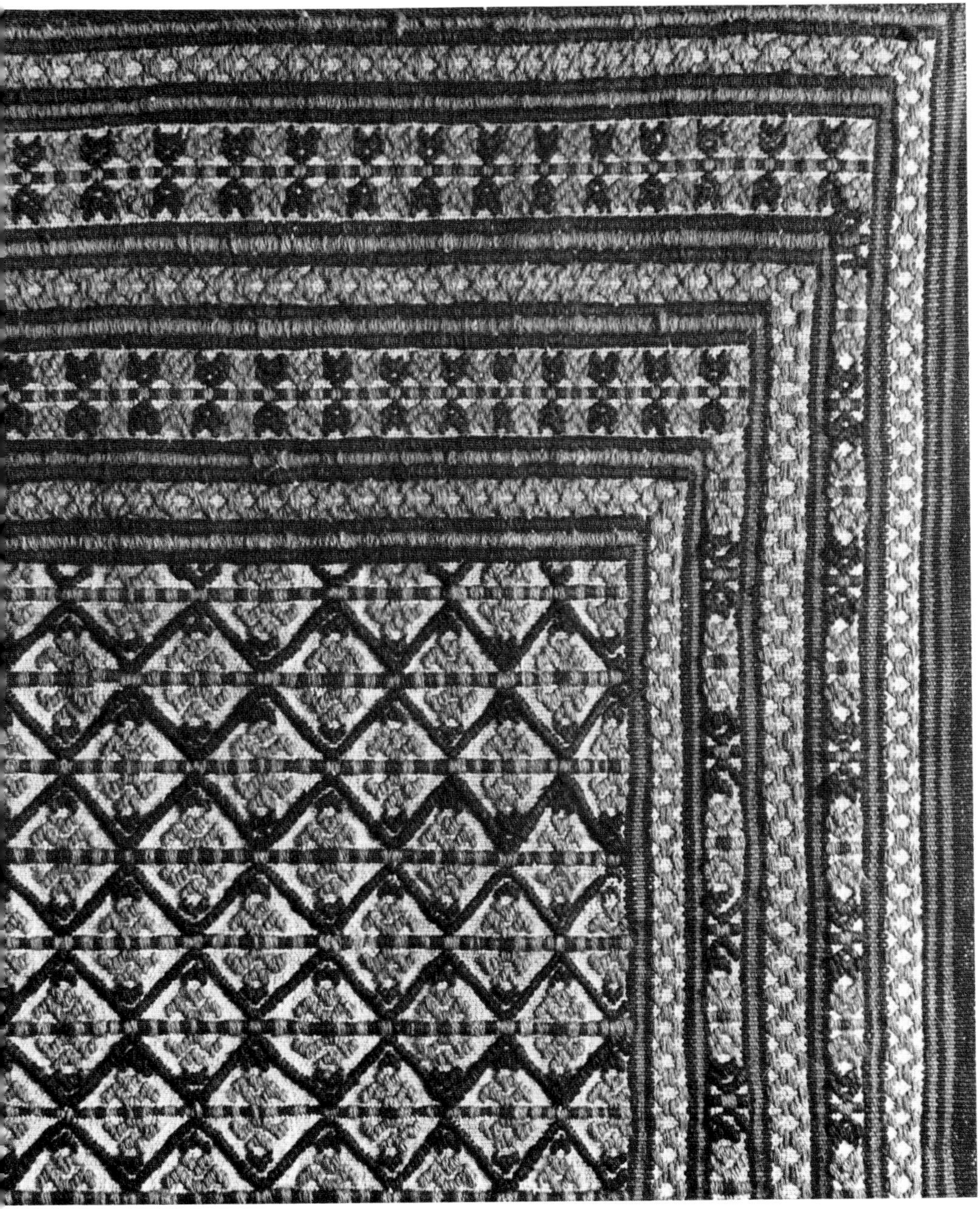

sketch in the design. The usual paint mediums will work, but it is wise to spray gloss the warp cloth before painting. The paints should be on the dry side, rather than creamy. If you plan to leave some warp cloth bare of wool, the best way to apply your design is sewing thread. Baste or running stitch the design with the appropriate colors in cotton sewing thread. They can be snipped out as you work your design.

When the project is finished, steam block it after tacking it down dry. Place the tacks at least an inch from the work. If it needs more than just steam, tack it out and then lay a wet sheet over it for a few hours and then let it dry. The stitching on this kind of cloth must be quite relaxed, if there is too much tension the material will just pucker up.

A warp cloth rug has to be lined if it is to have any body at all. An even weave cotton cloth, another strip of warp cloth, mattress ticking or denim will all serve. Miss Larsen's rubber triangles in the corners will prevent its slipping around on the floor. There are two ways of lining warp cloth depending on whether you plan to fringe or not. If you don't plan a fringe, a warp cloth rug can be lined just the way a canvas rug is, tack-quilting the lining to the rug, and then blind-stitching the two pieces together. If you plan to fringe, sew by hand or by machine one mesh out from the needlework with the right sides of rug and lining facing each other. The seam should go almost all the way around the rug. Leave enough unsewn so that you can turn the rug right side out, then blind-stitch the remaining way. Before you turn it, however, trim the excess cloth and lining away to within a half inch of the work. Snip the corners a trifle closer. After you have turned the rug, press it flat in the corners and along the edge with a damp cloth and iron.

Work a couple of rows of Turkey work over and under that empty row of mesh, one row should go next to the needlework and one row next to the lining. Trim the fringe and you are finished.

If you are quite sure that the wools are color-fast, a warp cloth rug should be quite washable. Before you wash it, firmly baste

Mrs. Christian Herter worked this rug for her husband, the seal is the Secretary of State's. It was worked on fourteen mesh canvas which allowed Mrs. Herter to have more detail in the design.

some white twill tape along the edges (over the fringe). After the rug is washed the tape will serve as tacking strips so that stretch holes will not occur in the body of the rug when you block it. The tapes save you from having to take the lining off, they are removed when the rug is dry.

INDEX OF STITCHES

BIBLIOGRAPHY

LIST OF SUPPLIERS

# Index of Stitches

# Bibliography

ALLARD, MARY, *Rug Making, Techniques and Design,* New York: Chilton Books, 1963

BOWLES, ELLA SHANNON, *Handmade Rugs,* New York: Garden City Publishing Company, 1937

FARADAY, CORNELIA BATEMAN, *European and American Carpets and Rugs,* Grand Rapids, Michigan: The Dean-Hicks Company, 1929

GIBBON, M. A., *Canvas Work,* London: G. Bell and Sons, Ltd., 1965

HAWLEY, WALTER A., *Oriental Rugs Antique and Modern,* New York: Dover Publications Inc., 1970 edition

HOLT, ROSA BELLE, *Oriental & Occidental Rugs Antique & Modern,* New York: Garden City Publishing Company, 1937

JACOBSEN, CHARLES W., *Oriental Rugs, A Complete Guide,* Tokyo: Rutland: Charles Tuttle Company, Inc., 1962

LANDREAU, ANTHONY N. & PICKERING, W. R., *From the Bosporus to Samarkand: Flat-Woven Rugs,* Washington, D. C.: The Textile Museum, 1969

MACBETH, ANN, *The Country Woman's Rug Book,* Peoria, Illinois: The Manual Arts Press, 1936

ROTH, RODRIS, *18th Century Floor Coverings in America,* Washington, D. C.: Smithsonian Press, 1967

THOMAS, MARY, *Mary Thomas's Dictionary of Embroidery Stitches,* London: Hodder & Stoughton, 1965

WALKER, LYDIA LE BARON, *Homecraft Rugs,* New York: Frederick A. Stokes Company, 1929

WEEKS, JEANNE G., AND TREGANOWAN, DONALD, *Rugs & Carpets of Europe and the Western World,* Philadelphia: Chilton Book Company, 1969

WHEELER, CANDACE THURBER, *How To Make Rugs,* Doubleday Page, 1902

WILLIAMS, ELSA, *Bargello Florentine Canvas Work,* New York: Reinhold Publishing Corporation, 1967

WILLIAMS, MODDIE JEFFRIES, *A Primer of Facts About Oriental Rugs,* New York; Carleton Press, 1967

WISEMAN, ANN, *Rag Tapestries and Wool Mosaics,* New York; Van Nostrand Reinhold Company, 1969

*Turkish Rugs,* edited by Ralph S. Yohe and H. McCoy Jones, An exhibition of the Washington Hajji Baba, Washington, D. C., The Textile Museum, 1968

STAINED GLASS

ARNOLD, HUGH, *Stained Glass of the Middle Ages in England* and France, London: Adam and Charles Black, 1913

BEYER, VICTOR, *Stained Glass Windows,* Edited by David Talbot Rice, Translated by M. von Herzfeld and R. Gaze, London: Oliver and Boyd, 1964

# List of Suppliers

THE following firms will be able to supply your local shop with the materials mentioned in this book. Paternayan Brothers and Handwork Tapestries sell wholesale only.

PATERNAYAN BROTHERS, INC.      Canvas and wools
312 East 95th Street
New York, N.Y., 10028

HANDWORK TAPESTRIES   Canvas and Bon Pasteur wools
3389 Colony Drive
Baldwin, N.Y., 11510

WILLIAMS MANUFACTURING COMPANY
West Townsend, Massachusetts, 01474

SCANDINAVIAN ART HANDICRAFT
7696 Camargo Road, Madeira
Cincinnati, Ohio, 45243

NANTUCKET NEEDLEWORKS
Nantucket Island, Massachusetts, 02554

EMILE BERNAT & SONS
Depot and Mendon Streets
Uxbridge, Massachusetts, 01569